BA182T
Ackerman, Diane.
Twilight of the ten ern memoir
A   ocm05777090

19019200068 1855

W9-BDA-628

BA182t

Ackerman.

Twilight of the tenderfoot.

NO LONGER PROPERTY
OF EASTON AREA
PUBLIC LIBRARY
Easton, PA 18042

1980

Twilight
of the
Tenderfoot

BY DIANE ACKERMAN

Twilight of the Tenderfoot: A Western Memoir

Wife of Light

The Planets: A Cosmic Pastoral

Twilight of the Tenderfoot

A Western Memoir

by Diane Ackerman

Easton Area Public Library
6th & Church Sts.
Easton, PA. 18042

WILLIAM MORROW AND COMPANY, INC.
New York   1980

BA 182 t

Copyright © 1980 by Diane Ackerman

All photographs by Paul Todesco

All rights reserved. No part of this book may be reproduced or utilized in any form or by any means, electronic or mechanical, including photocopying, recording or by any information storage and retrieval system, without permission in writing from the Publisher. Inquiries should be addressed to William Morrow and Company, Inc., 105 Madison Ave., New York, N. Y. 10016.

Library of Congress Cataloging in Publication Data

Ackerman, Diane.
  Twilight of the tenderfoot.

  1. Tequesquite Ranch, N. M.   2. Ranch life—New Mexico—Tequesquite Ranch.   3. New Mexico—Social life and customs.
4. Ackerman, Diane—Biography.   5. Poets, American—20th century—Biography.   I. Title.
F804.T35A27   978.9′24   79-25181
ISBN 0-688-03605-8

Printed in the United States of America

First Edition

1 2 3 4 5 6 7 8 9 10

Book Design by Michael Mauceri

APR 2 4 1980

Acknowledgments

This book is fondly dedicated to Albert J. and Sherrie Mitchell and their family, who welcomed the stranger I was with generosity and affection, and made my stays on the Tequesquite a charm as well as an education. And also to the cowhands and staff of the Tequesquite, whose work sometimes doubled when I was "helping out," and whose humor could make arduous days a treat.

I am grateful to *WomenSports* for first publishing parts of the book. Some of the photographs were exhibited in the Johnson Art Museum on the Cornell University campus.

Thanks to Gregory Kolovakos for his help with some Spanish idioms; and Christopher Bull to whom I am indebted for more reasons than I have space to say.

Preface

My earliest recollection is being fear-struck and three, trotting around a corral on the back of *something* steamy and rough gaited when, grabbing bristly mane in a panic, I glanced behind me and saw a brown rump speckled with loud white spots, each spot crazier and more circusy than the next. The horse must have been an appaloosa (from the Nez Percé, who bred them along the Palouse River). The bristly black mane comes with the genetic suit as do the striped hooves, a sickly white sclera circling the eyes, and (books never tell you this) speckled genitals and nostrils.

Since then, I've ridden horses steadily through the years: with lessons, without lessons; on the flat, jumping fences; outside in the drizzles of autumn, in riding halls blacker than a sump. What lures me still is the disciplined panic of a horse flirting with a tantrum at every turn, the delicate, voluptuous play of muscles, the grace-sprung power.

All my childhood's Saturday mornings I devoted to the Lone Ranger, Roy Rogers, and the Cisco Kid, and was rhapsodic when TV shows such as "Fury" or "My Friend Flicka" came along. Even now, I can't eat a Fig Newton without thinking of the Southwest and "Sky King." And every Saturday afternoon, I picked my way through tall grass and unknown neighborhoods to that dark, broody stable on the outskirts of town and respectable life, there to trade 50¢ for an hour's ride. When eventually the stable language grew so bad, and the men who ran the place so seedy, that my mother brought a sudden halt to my barn visits, it was as if the stuffing had been butted out of me. I cried undistractably. Mother was surprised, a little frightened even, that a child so young could hurt so deeply over the loss of what was, after all, only a pastime. I got my way, and headed straight back to the stable. For me, there were no riding rings and decaying barn-slats, no geezers leaning drunkenly against a tackroom door, only the thrill of a headlong gallop on the flat, cactus-strewn prairie I'd seen in all those westerns. In rural Illinois, where the land is flat as a penny, my mesas were yardless housing tracts and, beyond them, the orange bulldozers parked in neat, even rows against the horizon.

Twenty years later, a full-grown earth-ecstatic and a poet, I decided one day to write *An Esthetics of the Horse*. Where, I asked a local horsetrader, if anywhere, do they still cowboy like they used to? An old question. And he told me about a large, working cattle ranch in northeastern New Mexico, that Albert J. Mitchell ran, adding that the "Tequesquite" had been in the Mitchell family for eighty-one years, and that it was an old-fashioned ranch where calves were bred, raised, and fattened for slaughter in much the same ways they were years ago in the Old West.

One spring day I sent a candid letter to Albert Mitchell, asking if I might join his cowboys during branding season to see what they still did on horses. Back came an answer full of hospitality; I could feel him smiling in the margins. Surely he thought the notion a little strange at best, but he was game. So in June, 1977, I flew from my home in Ithaca, New York, to Amarillo, Texas, rented a car, and drove three hours west to the 180,000-acre Tequesquite Ranch in Albert, New Mexico. I asked Mitchell and his foreman, at all costs, not to pamper me, but let me ride with the cowhands, working exactly as they did, whatever that might entail. At 5:30 the next morning, I buckled on my chaps, and rode out to herd cattle for the first time in my life, not knowing exactly what I would find in an American past mine only by association, a landscape alien as Mars, a desert heat and physical labor so hard it leaves you aching all over.

Where I journeyed from, the sun had a three-hour headstart, but somehow the time gap felt like more than a century. Amaze me, teach me, I ask even of the hibiscus in the garden; how could I not ask it of so alien a way of life? What happened to me on the Tequesquite I've not yet recovered from; even now, in the comfort of my woodsy home in Ithaca, where lilac sweetly leadens the air and the whole yard's a-twitch, I'm tempted to leave my family, my job, my habits, and fly off to explore, say, a coral reef (driven not by an adventurer's longing, but a naturalist's).

"Home is where the heart remembers/Having been its oldest version," a friend writes in an early poem. And some days, without warning, I leave the present behind me in a wake of mental dust, appear on an ancient African savannah, and *become* Neanderthal watching the day begin from a cool, damp cave, thinking, perhaps for the first time so abstractly, how clean, how silky, how fine the air feels compared with yesterday and the humid days before it; or, finding an elephant print at the waterhole whose clay walls are sunbaked almost to pottery, notice the water trapped inside, and *feel* what it must have felt like to first realize how useful a portable version of that footprint would be.

For all my flagrant intensity, I always find life denser and more colorful than I expect. How will I ever know it all, the lavish, eruptive here-and-now, let alone the whims of evolution and culture that somehow led to this woman on this patio full of geraniums? How many lifestyles would I have to experience to feel persuaded in old age that I had really known life?

Some worlds lie beyond my keenest imaginings: on the Tequesquite, I was amazed to see cowboying go on as it had for ages, and knew that I was witnessing the last moments of an exotic, swiftly vanishing way of life, one in the American grain and, I suppose, typically human. It's not so much that I shelved the *Esthetics of the Horse*, which I will, and must, write one day. From the minute I rode through the first pasture gate, and began loping among stinkweed, sagebrush and cactus, diamond-backed rattlers and low-nesting desert birds, on either side of me cowboys dressed in full regalia, chatting and riding unselfconsciously to work, the *Esthetics of the Horse* never entered my mind. I joined the ranch with the rapt gusto of a tenderfoot, returning in each of its seasons to learn its pulse and style as best I could. One rarely has the chance to sample the landscape of one's heart's desire; what follows is a prose version of that country.

Twilight
of the
Tenderfoot

PART I

Branding Season

June

1

Driving west of Amarillo, I notice cattle grazing along the runway, and endless, flat, wheat-gold fields over which the blue sky pales away to white. In the background are machines, factories, twentieth-century artifacts, but in the foreground five or six horses munch sagebrush and mesquite, a windmill whirls swiftly in the breeze, and, everywhere, barbed wire fences stretch to the horizon. What with the scrub brush, the long trenchy culverts, and a glaring sun that seems to reduce things to their structural minimums (horses look like kindergarten drawings: a few rough dark lines), I feel as if I'm watching "The Cisco Kid," or "The Westerners," as if the Saturday mornings of my childhood, full of black-hatted desperadoes, sexless cowboys, and universal values free from any extenuating circumstance or compromise, have come back to haunt me. I pass a road sign announcing SPUR 48, by which they undoubtedly mean spur-route, not an exhortation to a ranch hand, but I find it odd in this country where every other store and gas station seems to be named Hi-Plains

Grocery or Panhandle Dry Cleaners, and recall how the Budget Rent-a-Car girl had shown up in a pair of snug jogging shorts, halter top, and Dr. Scholl sandals. The radio station she tapped rhythm to on the steering wheel played locally flavored rock songs like "Southern Nights" and "Marie from Amarillo" (obviously a favorite) between advertisements for fast-food chains and car franchises. Amarillo she had pronounced in a drawl as "Emerald."

The little settlements all look temporary, as if they have been thrown up carelessly in the night, and won't be needed long. Even the large ranch houses, all of which are one-story, seem to suggest a contractor who, going bankrupt, never quite got round to adding-on the second floor. Already, the air is 95° F, but so dry that I'm comfortable in my long-sleeved sweater whose rainbow stripes look like the rind of some exotic fruit. Casting long, subdued shadows, the sun sparkles on aluminum siding or chrome bumpers, and makes the dark, freshly ploughed fields, crusted with buff tones, bake like an enormous mincemeat pie. Never have I seen so many long golden fields.

Between two mesas, I come upon a road sign that warns of "Dangerous Crosswinds," and, with visions of being swept up in a funnel, I slow the car to a discreet 50 m.p.h. The clay soil is salmon colored, Martian, but the woolliness of the scrub brush and the weathered, wind-tormented trees remind me less of the *Viking* photos of Mars than of Israel. All along Highway 40, flat-topped mesas pour into one another, now like breaking waves, and now like a Sphinx inching forward on its stone haunches. Another road sign reads "Please Help Prevent Grass Fire." And right next to it: "Keep Your Curves. Eat More Texas Beef." Far away—perhaps five miles, or perhaps a hundred—I see a string of mesas. Up north I'd be looking at the sharp, interfolding Alleghenies; here the mountains look lopped off, planed flat for some as-yet-undisclosed masonry.

What a cruel harsh country this must have been for the turn-of-the-century cowboy; it sprawls unbroken through inedible scrub, cracked dirt, and ever-whitening grass. The sunlight is so bright it makes objects dance in a carnival vapor, which is perhaps why police cars, every so often, lurk in the cool shade of the occasional tree. The blue sky is everywhere, and, for a moment, I feel as if I'm driving into the ocean. Tufted as it is with spiky cacti and yucca plants and low kelpy sagebrush, the open prairie looks for all the world like a sea bottom. There are no fish on this reef, and the air is so dry it peppers the throat, but the shape of landfall is oceanic.

By the time I reach the tiny settlement called Logan, I've had a long lush drink of the prairie. I stop in at one of the town's two bars to pick up a bottle of Jack Daniel's for my hosts, the Mitchells. The woman-bartender wipes a thick layer of dust from the shoulders of the bottle, and quips that I'm getting a little New Mexico real estate for free. Outside, things look stark in the white-hot early-morning sun. Even the crows look blacker. The subtle blends of talcy color along the mesas are devastatingly beautiful, a pastel apparition. Like Impressionist paintings, subtle-hued and vapory, they line the valley, the turbulence of whose landscape is heart-revving. Here and there, in a dried-up riverbed, a sudden luminous pool of water lies like a piece of slate. *A piece of water* I recall from Clint Eastwood westerns. Once, in New York City's Museum of Modern Art, I saw an exhibition of American Romanticism, and was struck by the rougey transparencies of light, which I assumed were a stylistic quirk. Now I understand what captivated those painters, and how doggedly realistic their lightings were. On my left, a cherry-red mesa rises steeply. The landscape is so intense and dramatic, it seizes you from moment to moment, grabs you by the lapels, shakes you hard, and says, "Wake up! Live!" And, in that earthly seizure, *land* becomes as eternal and persuasive as any abstraction.

When I reach the main gate of the Tequesquite Ranch, I'm still seven miles from the core buildings (or "headquarters," as they're called). On all sides, the ranch is buffeted by mesas, some of them the most colorful I've seen, Christmasy: clay-red dirt splattered with green brush. I continue driving, but, twenty minutes later, still have not reached the main camp. Wildflowers cry out in delicate clumps of bright yellow, blue, and purple blossoms riding low, like jockeys in their silks, over the brown land. Suddenly a cow, grazing by the road-side, darts in front of me, its long horns menacing. And then it dawns on me that the cow is not tightly enclosed, but running wild as any antelope or coyote. I feel like a tornado, leaving my white dusty wake behind me; in a pothole, I nearly leave my axle as well. So many adobe houses and trailer homes rise up, I don't know exactly which one to head for, so, pulling into a yard full of children and chickens and yapping dogs, I ask a Spanish woman where the men might be branding. She points toward some invisible distance, and says, "See those trucks there?" Squinting, I pick out the shape of something shiny in the far glitter of the June sun. She says, "They're out thatta way," as if she were saying, "Next door." And so, with a relative notion of "thatta way," I climb into my car and follow the dirt road back to the pavement, and the pavement out farther into the plains. Casually, I glance into my rearview mirror, and am startled to see the road fleeing into a sunlit mesa. On the highway just ahead, four buzzards fly off from their road kill. And then some *thing* becomes visible, some vision that might be a herd of pickup trucks. I head toward it, my pulse gathering like a storm.

Out of the brush, a barbed wire corral appears, full of noisy cattle, moaning like the damned, boys, cowhands, and impromptu branding-fires. A dusty cowboy comes toward me with a grin that has no doubt sized up my clean eastern garb, notebook, and camera, my purple-frame sunglasses and round-toed boots.

"Albert Mitchell?" I ask tentatively. He stretches a dark, suntanned arm across the barbed wire, greets me shyly, then introduces me to his three sons (home from school to help with branding), his foreman, and top hands. I forget each name as it's presented to me, losing it between the Spanish surnames and the southwestern accent. Then, too, the faces look alike: glazed with dirt and sweat, sunburnt, eyes ringed dark as coal miners'. All their chaps are oily and blood splattered, their western hats pulled down low over their foreheads. But Al's voice is steady as a lightning conductor and, at the same time, full of wry poise; you can almost see the commas hanging in the air, so lackadaisical is his drawl.

"Come on in," he says, and offers me a hand to help me climb over the barbed wire fence. But there's a knack to climbing barbed wire, and it takes two men and five clumsy minutes, during which I feel embarrassingly uninitiated, to swing me over the spiky fence unharmed.

It happens that a dozen or so boys from The Boys Ranch, a New Mexico home for boys, have been on the ranch all week, being trained as ranch hands. All around the small corral, they are either resting or "flanking" (wrestling) cattle, carrying the "nutbucket," in which the testicles are tossed after castration, and generally helping out while keeping out of the way. The Boys Ranch boys are, as Al's wife, Sherrie, says, "gutty little guys," who are hard working, well mannered, and apparently grateful for the vacation. In addition to feeding and housing them (they spend most evenings frolicking on the ranch trampoline), the Mitchells are paying them a salary, and it seems to please them especially to be taken seriously as hands. Most importantly, Al Mitchell is teaching them a trade. Often, in the thick of the corral hubbub, I see him take a moment to teach one of them a little flanking finesse, or, for that matter, give tips to his regular hands. The boys flock round me, the *rara avis* in their midst, and are endless, almost pesky, founts of questions. But they are sweet, polite, and cute (many of them Spanish Americans with large dark eyes), spunky, and ravenous for affection. I chat with them nonstop most of the first afternoon. We talk about The Boys Ranch, which is run strictly by donation, and houses boys whose parents have deserted them, and yet will not allow them to be put up for adoption, young boys in a painful limbo, for whom The Boys Ranch staff tries to provide training, discipline, and love. The houseparents are dedicated, hard working, and poorly paid. One of them, Don, grew up on The Boys Ranch himself, and now lives there with his wife. The other housefather I met, Stan, is an ex-preacher who believes in health food and diligence, and somehow manages a balance of strict discipline and generous affection. Both of the housefathers (whom the boys call "dad") know cowboying, and spend the branding days working as hard as any of the regular hands, as do the boys, who grow lobster-faced and enervated from the all-out exertion and searing, unbreathable air.

I take a seat on the fence rail to keep out of the way, and feel a little guilty seated high on the top beam of the corral, as if on Olympus, while so much sweat and labor happens below me. Everything is distracting, salient, new. The cowboys are all shy of me, taciturn and wary. I don't know where to spend my attention first.

A young handsome cowboy tugs down his hatbrim, then rides straight into the clustering cattle, swinging his rope round in wide perfect loops, then catches up the back leg of a mother-snuggling calf, churns his horse round, and bolts a few yards until the rope yanks taut and the calf stumbles to the ground. He drags it yammering into the center of the ring. There a "flanking team," two cowboys, wrestle the struggling calf to the ground, one grappling with the calf's head and neck, and the other with its back legs. The front cowboy folds back one foreleg, as if to snap it off, then rocks all of his weight against it, while the rear cowboy sits on the ground at the calf's rump, one foot on the inside thigh of the animal, the other calf-leg at full stretch in his hands. Mitchell holds a razory knife high in the air, so as not to cut anyone inadvertently, as he walks toward the flanked calf to begin castrating and ear-cutting. First he slices the calf's ear at a steep angle, which means it's a female calf (the males' ears are only bobbed at the tip), and stuffs the piece of cut-off ear into the pocket of his chaps. At day's end, Mitchell will remove the bits from his chaps pockets and, laying them out on the front seat of a pickup truck, know at a glance how many calves were branded that day, as well as how many of them were male and how many female. Slicing the ears differently benefits the cowhand, who can then tell at a distance what animal he is dealing with, and also serves as an additional way of branding. Next Mitchell castrates the calf, though from where I sit I cannot see the operation. In fact, all the calves to be castrated are flanked with their backs toward me the first day. I know, given the dusty ruckus of the branding ring, such a plan could not possibly be premeditated, and wonder if, subconsciously, they may be trying to avoid shocking my delicate eastern sensibility. Mitchell's ten-year-old daughter, Lynda, who, with her sun-tinted complexion and dutch-girl hairdo, looks like she skipped out of a painting by Vermeer, already knows much about the land and animals. Leaning toward me from her perch on a lower fence rail, she refers to the job matter-of-factly as "steering." And on my other side, deaf to Lynda's remark in all the noise, a young Boys Rancher, his processes confused, describes it as "circumcising" the calf. Mitchell takes an instrument from the hand of a nutbucket carrier, and what he does with the gleaming, wrench-shaped "masculators" is lost to my view. He drops two silvery bullet-shaped testicles into the bucket, then takes a small black canister and sprays the raw area with disinfectant.

But while Mitchell is cutting, other things are happening

all over the calf. A cowboy wielding a blunt pipelike knife rubs it against the calf's incipient horn, razoring the growth away in a rise of blood. Then another cowhand applies a long, red-hot poker to the dehorned area to cauterize the wound and prevent the horn's regrowth. On the left jowl, the brander burns a **K** in three careful strokes, skating the branding iron smoothly through the fur, while he holds the calf's snout steady with his bootheel. Two cowboys administer two injections, one against blackleg, the other a solid dose of vitamin A. Finally, a hand injects a pellet of synthetic hormone just under the skin at the ear, to help the calf grow faster.

"WHOOOAH," the calves bellow as they're being branded. "OHHHH," as their horns are sliced off, leaving behind a button of shiny bright blood. The ear-marking seems not to bother them much. Some defecate as they're being held, and the cowboys' chaps are all splattered with excrement and blood. I wince at the burning jowl flesh under the branding iron, am chilled by the secret operation in the calf's groin.

A struggling calf bolts free before the cowboys have finished with it, and, grinning, one of the boys leaps after it, being dragged along the fence, and finally wrestling its 300 pounds of panic to the ground. The calf's eye rolls, its nostrils swell and puff, and its tongue roams aimlessly about its mouth as it yammers, "WHOOAH," "OHHHHH."

"Hey, burn this horn here," a flanker yells. And, one foot on the calf's squirming snout, a cowboy plants the long beveled iron straight down on the velvet, singeing it, leaving behind a small black crater. The stench of burnt horns turns my stomach. The calf's eye is white and translucent. I am as dazed as any of these dumb beasts to see cowboying happen here in the third third of the twentieth century, just as it happened a hundred years ago, while the *Viking* spacecraft sends back color photos of Mars. The only difference I detect is the herd of pickup trucks, and the branding irons fired red-hot by two butane tanks which flush fire into a metal trough. My attention roams, and I realize that all over the corral the same scene is unfolding. Three or four calves are being flanked at once.

Al's son Tom continues roping from the back of a palomino, his rapt features moving decisively from thought to thought as, loop in hand, he dodges after a skittish calf, his movements so confident, so corral-wise, it's hard to believe that he's only seventeen, and that, underneath that mask of dust, strain, and sweat, are pale eyebrows and a boyish face. When the rope yanks tight, he slides expertly into the side of the saddle, to avoid the sharp singing of the nylon against his waist, drags the calf bawling into the arena, tail first, its four legs beating the ground like canes.

An older hand, R. J., lifts a dusty canteen to his mouth as he walks toward me, and I watch his adam's apple ripple as he drinks. His neck and face are both deeply tanned, dark and leathery, his legs a little bowed, and his body long, lean, and wiry. Unconsciously, I break into a laugh.

"What's so funny?" he asks.

And I tell him that for a moment it was a hundred years ago. I was out on the range with a real cowboy sipping from a canteen. R. J. looks puzzled. He *is* a real cowboy. And he's working the same way he's worked for forty years. Only fifty-seven, he looks older from the sun, dust, and wind.

"Don't you ever get bored riding the range all day?" I ask him, as I ask most of the cowboys at one time or another during my stay.

"Sure ya' do," he says, "but you're bound to get bored if ya' keep at anything long enough." He lifts his injection gun, and inoculates the next calf.

Everything stops at lunchtime, when the hands drive out to the nearest waterhole to wash up in its round metal pool, and drink cool well water from the pipe. A tall windmill drives the pump, its blades flashing round in the ever-present breeze. Minus the hats casting shadows across their faces, and the mummifying layers of clotted dirt, sweat, and blood which make them look almost allegorical, like mimes in white-mask, the cowboys suddenly have features. Pleased, I take in the variety of eye shapes and colors, skin tones, cheek-bones (some steep as cliff rock), hair, wrinkles, degrees of calm. The hodgepodge of ages and ancestries makes an end-lessly distracting facial panorama, running from pale, straight-haired Germanic to walnut-skinned, curly-haired Spanish American, hitting all of the types in between.

Al, I notice, is of medium height and a little stocky, his muscles condensed like a quarter horse's into a strong, alert frame. His hands are large as a pianist's, though sunburnt and muscular. But it's his dark eyes, eloquent as those of an art dealer bidding at an auction, that rivet you. "Don't worry, it's okay," their gentle focus reassures a clumsy Boys Rancher; a steel glare to a cowboy tells him unambiguously what a repeat of his misdeed will mean; at the slightest joke, laugh lines crease each corner; when he's anxious, they seem pre-cariously neutral; at funny mishaps, they flash silent guffaws; when he's hugging Lynda, they relax in a swim of affection.

By the time we return to branding camp, the ranch women have arrived with an enormous lunch, which they carefully arrange on the back of a pickup truck. Usually, the lunch in-cludes fresh, solid beef (short ribs, for instance, or slabs of roast beef, or a heavy, savory meat loaf), Mexican beans with optional chili sauce (I break into a cold sweat just sniffing it), mashed potatoes and gravy, coleslaw or tossed salad, hot panfuls of homemade rolls, corn, broccoli, spinach, or some other vegetable, and then dessert, which might be peach cobbler, or lemon cake, or chocolate bread pudding. Three large thermoses hold iced tea, Kool-Aid, and water. In a large pale-blue chest, tiny cubes of ice are the ultimate luxury in this subduing heat. Overhead, the sun burns like white-hot cotton dipped in lye. So the cowboys take the opportunity to "shade" for a little while, that is, find shade to rest or eat lunch in. Often they lay their chaps under a pickup truck, and stretch out on them to rest, their hats tilted down over their eyes. Others eat lunch or rest in the cabs of the trucks, whose doors are left open to trap the breeze. The main thing is to get out of the direct sun for a short spell. My sandal-exposed toes are cut up from the prickly cacti and yuccas, my head aches from the sun that's as frantic as a siren, and my arms tingle in their silent burn. Already, I've begun to revise my habits, as I will do frequently during my stay; tomorrow I'll wear a hat, boots, and a long-sleeved shirt.

Between sips of water, Al introduces me to his wife, Sherrie, a lithe, handsome woman, who welcomes me with gracious good will. I ask her if she ever joins the hands in herding or branding.

"Riding, that isn't ma' bag," she says with a smile. Sherrie is the quiet center around which the ranch seems to pivot. She's sensitive to people the way Al is to the land and animals, knows when trouble's brewing, or when indulgence is needed. She is like the grand lady of a hacienda or plantation, which, of course, is precisely what she is. Hers is the Herculean task of orchestrating all of the ranch dwellers' lives. Not only the cowboys who live in the bunkhouse, but their married counterparts who have separate houses on the ranch; the women like Juanita and Porfia who attend the Mitchells in their house and double as cooks in a pinch; the usual cook; the school-teacher (children of the cowhands are educated on the ranch; sometimes the Mitchells even send them on to higher education); Rachel, a bright, pretty Spanish-American girl who cleans, acts as governess to Lynda, and is a resource person available for all manner of errand; groundsmen; and other assorted ranch workers, their spouses, their children, and their in-laws. Sherrie is responsible for all of them. She will feed them, house them, educate their families, see they get the proper medical attention, cuddle their children, cry over their misfortunes. She is no less the hub of their lives than the ranch is, and, like a hub, she holds them all steady.

After lunch, the branding resumes. Rachel's older brother, Mettie, gets up to rope on a horse that's new to roping and, consequently, unpredictable. Mettie whirls his rope around in those stiff perfect loops I've come to recognize and, aiming for the calf's ankle, misses it by a hair. On the second try, the rope nearly rips from his hands, so frantic are the horse's movements. Mettie is "dallying" the rope, not tying it fast to the saddle horn, but waiting until the calf is lassoed and the line pulled tight before winding the free end furiously around the saddle horn (sometimes lagged with rubber to make the rope stick), still managing somehow to hold the reins. It's a tougher way to rope than "tying fast," but safer; a bystander (in this case, one of The Boys Ranch boys) is less likely to get hurt in a tight trap of rope. This time, Mettie's toss catches up both of the calf's back legs and yanks them tight; he runs the free rope-end swiftly round the saddle horn, and with the other hand, controls the calf and guides his horse, which now begins to buck and spin in alarm. Silently, the crew moves toward him in unison, oblivious to their instinctive steps; but just as suddenly, Mettie pulls the horse out of its spin, and work continues as usual.

Mettie is beautiful in that rough, tough, Old West cowboy way: gnarled, scarred, bashful, and gutsy. The sort of cowboy the West was built by, and cowboy myths built around.

"Do you go into the city much?" I ask him during a rare lull in his duties.

"Sometimes, two or three times a month maybe. Depends how busy we are," he says, and in teasing understatement, adds, "Sometimes we're pretty busy."

"Don't you get lonely riding the range all day?" And instantly I feel ashamed for asking the sort of question only a spoiled eastern intellectual, used to a steady stream of films, books, and people, could not only pose, but *mean*. Ever to

be bored, as the poet John Berryman said, is to admit you
have no inner resources. I am ashamed, but I must ask such
a question just the same.

"Oh, you just think about the cows," Mettie says, "you
hope you won't find nothing sick or hurt. Sure, you leave
early in the morning and come back late, but I like it, I've
been doing that all my life. Anyway, a horse is a pretty good
friend." He grins.

"Yes," I agree, "it doesn't talk back, or want a prom
dress."

Given the high sign by Al, Mettie disappears into the
throng of churning cows.

There are about 200 horses on the ranch; the Mitchells
raise and break their own, turning out the mares and foals to
run free in a canyon, and keeping a close eye on the stallions,
while using the more manageable geldings for ranch work.
The cowboys' mounts, all quarter horses, are tightly muscled
and meticulously trained. They jump up the two feet into the
stock trailers without fuss. They stay put when the reins
are dropped straight down, even if they're out in the middle
of the prairie. They regard a loose drape of the reins over a
fence rail as a permanent arrangement. They neck-rein at the
slightest touch. They endure all sorts of whoops and hollers
and whistles, smacking ropes and flashing hats without flinch-
ing. They ride straight at obstreperous bulls without shying.
They weave among the mesquite, cacti, and yucca, or clip
through them at full gallop, with no complaint. They move
calmly among frantic cows in dust-thick corrals full of burning smells, bellowing, and hot irons. They turn adroitly and
gamely to herd stray cattle. They break into a lope with
little persuasion. Heads dropped to nearly the level of their
backs, they trot evenly over long distances. They are well
tuned and remarkably sound for all the stress that must be
placed on their legs in those fast tight turns and sudden jumps

at odd angles. One thing especially charms me: when a horse is riderless, he arches his tail as he canters, as if it were a flag of his freedom. These horses, as I notice riding the range the next day, arch their tails automatically as they lope, rider or no rider, across the open prairie.

The cowboys, who by now have finished with one herd of cattle, and have begun to round up a second herd, see me in the car making notes, and contrive to drive the new herd straight at me. They all begin to wink and smile, knowing of course that the cows will part and go around me, as if I were a small obstruction in an artery, but *I* have no such inside information, and am panic-stricken the car will be gashed and overturned. In the middle of this contained stampede, all I can think of is death by trampling. I smile, and try to act unruffled, though my knees are quaking. I can see the headlines.

Come nightfall, I bunk with Rachel, who lives alone in a well-furnished, three-bedroom trailer near the schoolhouse. But her evenings she frequently spends visiting with her brothers. There are nine Gutierrez children, and all of them have worked at the ranch at one time or another. The youngest, whom Sherrie affectionately calls "Little Britches," sleeps in the bunkhouse during branding week, and works with the cowboys. Coming from a close-knit family, out of a close-knit New Mexico town, Rachel seems to be at home in this equally close ranch-family life. But there isn't an abundance of young men when one is living on such an enormous spread so far out on the plains. Still, people manage to meet and get married; how, I'm not sure anyone quite knows.

Hot, sweaty, and spent from simply being on my feet all day under so wicked a desert sun, I set two tag-team alarm clocks, and station them at persuasive distances around the room, then tumble into bed. At 4:30, a time of day I take on faith, having never actually witnessed it firsthand before, I crawl out of bed, feeling as if I haven't had two hours of sleep to rub together. I pull back a drape, whose presence I didn't notice the night before, and am startled by the sudden eerie brilliance of a mesa, flat as a watercolor and shimmery on the horizon.

2

Everyone drives. The ranch has its own squad of pony-sized pickup trucks. Even little Lynda knows how to shift the automatic stick into drive, and stretch her toes down to the gas pedal and brake. Of course, there's nothing to hit. No stoplights or intersections. Just an occasional culvert or a cow. And the embarrassment I feel is beyond description when, on a dirt road in the middle of nowhere, I automatically flick on my turn signal. "Ackerman," I sigh, "you're like a trained seal."

Two minutes later, I'm at the cookhouse, joining a gaggle of sleepy-eyed cowboys, who are frying eggs in half an inch of bacon grease, munching bowls of cereal, eating stacks of buttered toast. They look amused when I sit down to drink coffee with them. Conversation stops instantly. We all eat in silence, return our cutlery to the sink, and head for the corral to fetch our horses.

"Ya' awake?" Al calls from a sea of quarter horses. He catches one, and begins to bridle it.

"Nope," I yell back, "I'm still in bed."

"You'll need a hat this morning," he advises me.

Feeling puckish, I answer by strutting into view with my farm-store-bought straw hat, and my flaming purple chaps. Al takes one look, shakes his head, and says, "Whew, those are some chaps." I can hear him chuckling softly as he runs a curry comb in even sweeps over the horse's rump.

My purple chaps (which the cowboys pronounce *sh*aps) are a dude's all right: clean, flashy, and impractical. Mine have white buck-stitching, in fancy metaphysical circles on each thigh instead of pockets good for keeping calf ears and fence tools. Back East, of course, pockets aren't needed for indoor riding, especially not for jumping. My chaps I acquired seriously, to prevent the terrible bruising my hunt-seat riding often led to, but they *are* colorful, a poet's chaps: deep, royal purple, with purple fringes that, as you walk, ripple like a flame. In contrast, the cowboys' chaps are oily, blood-splattered, ripped here and there by a snag of barbed wire, or an unexpected horn, and equipped with large, useful pockets, in which, among other things, cowboys often carry Chapstick.

"Those are pretty slick lady's chaps," Mike says. His own pair he made himself. Cowboy chaps (an abbreviation of *chaparejos*, Spanish for "leather leggings") are made of plain thick leather that buckles or zips down the back of each leg. The leather belt, on which the leg panels hinge, buckles at the back of the waist (the Mitchell boys have their names tooled into the leather here), and ties with a low-slung lace in the front.

By 6:00, we ride out of the gate like a posse, and weave through the endless yucca and cacti. Little Lynda, who's cute as her "Sugarplum" nickname, but often shockingly mature, expert, and resourceful, counsels me about rattlesnakes, impromptu bull fights, and the general how-to of cattle herding. Then the group splits up: Tom, Lynda, and I peel off to the right, and trot swiftly toward a bunch of grazing cattle in the distance. It's a rough trot over such broken terrain and, though I'm used normally to sitting a trot when I'm riding western style, I mimic Tom's position and rise forward in my stirrups instead, grabbing the saddle horn with a free hand. Back East, this maneuver would be considered "bad form"; here one hasn't time for such frippery. Good form is what works, and what works is what keeps you comfortably in the saddle. This does; and, like Tom, I occasionally post, or rock forward and grab the saddle horn, or sit squarely in the saddle, as we pace swiftly toward the cows. My horse, Prince, a ten-year-old gelding, is willing, mild mannered, and spooky (he refuses to sidle up to a fence, stay tied, or be caught without a few minutes' squabble). I like his feisty personality, which I find in no way off-putting, and am delighted when, as I fret his side lightly with my legs, he sweeps into a long, easy lope.

But something disturbs me that I can't pin down. And then it comes to me: I am out on the prairie where there are no walls. This is not a riding hall, whose end, final as a life, I will come to. I am riding freely across the open range in the same mythic West that salted my childhood with its six-shooting cowboys and burly desperadoes, and, just in front of me, is a herd of cattle to be driven to the waterhole.

Tom angles off to gather up a few barely visible strays. Lynda rides straight at the cows, whooping and hollering so frantically she sounds possessed.

"*Whoooooop! Oooo-a-oooop!*" she cries, over and over like a panicky loon, "*Whooop! Whooop!*"

From another quadrant, I hear someone else wailing. Tom has his own cry that sounds lower-pitched. And, spotting a recalcitrant calf dead in front of me, I gamely ride up, clear my throat, and whisper, "*whoop.*" The calf looks at me in disbelief. Certainly it doesn't move. Swinging my horse around in a wide even circle, I come at the calf again, wondering if perhaps I shouldn't try to reason with it. Instead, I

warble a falsetto "*Ooo-ooop!*" and the calf trots into the herd.
Drunk with my success, I chase up other dawdling cattle, my
hollers growing progressively bolder. I warm to the sport of
second-guessing the cow's movement, and pressing it quietly
into the herd. Mid-morning, left to drive the rear of the herd,
while Tom and Lyn chase roaming bulls on either side, I can't
resist what I've come out West to say.

"Gitta-long!" I yell with a grin broad as a legend. "Gitta-
long little doggie!" On cue, a straggling doggie spins around
and gits a-long.

It's only later, at the waterhole, as we relax in the saddle,
that I realize how achy my legs are from the morning's nine-
mile ride. Drawing one leg up around the saddle horn, I mas-
sage a knot growing just under the knee. But otherwise I feel
fine, exhilarated.

"How was your ride?" Russell, the soft-spoken foreman,
asks, as if I'd just returned from a quiet jog down a bridle
path in Central Park. Russell is handsome as a model, but no
more so than his wife, Delois, is pretty. A cowboy all his life,
and the son of a still-practicing cowboy, he met his wife at a
rodeo dance on one of his weekends off. Atop a horse in his
dusty garb and pointy boots, he looks as if he ambled straight
out of a Hollywood western.

"Ya' invest in some pretty chaps, didja?" Russell asks, his
eyes twinkling.

"I got them from a gay gaucho," I answer quietly, and wait
for the thunderclap.

"Wh-what was that?"

I repeat myself.

"That's just what I thought ya' said!" His face explodes
with a laugh.

My hat keeps rising and, on the morning's ride, actually
flew off once. I can't figure how the cowboys keep their hats
on in all the hubbub and desert wind. Finally, I secure the
sweatband under my browbone, and bend the rim down,

Australian-style, on one side. Underfoot, the dirt burns hotly through my boots. The cows sound like opera singers warming up, "Me, me, me, me, me." Outside the corral, a hobbled horse hops a few hundred feet.

"Did I spook your horse?" I ask Al, as his horse jumps wide at the gate, almost bashing him into the fence.

"He's not all that used to people coming up suddenly behind him," Al says in a gentle rebuke. And I make a mental note to be more careful; a half-ton of horse can be dangerous.

When the day's branding begins around 10:00, I notice that many of the cows already wear a ⊘ brand (referred to as "circle-slash"), which means they are unregistered. The registered calves (the bulls were monitored) are branded with the Tequesquite Ranch's brand: K ⊼ (a throwback to the original ranch owner, and Al's great-grandfather, a German immigrant named Knell).

Terry Mitchell does a lot of the branding today, even though he has a broken collarbone. Al Mitchell has two black-and-blue toes, and recently underwent knee surgery. Mettie, I notice, has an array of burns on his hands, and a few sizable cuts on his arm from barbed wire. But nobody complains, just as no one complains about the heat or hard work. Part of the cowboy code of honor is not to admit to pain. One day I ask the local veterinarian about this stoicism, and he tells me that Al Mitchell's father, Albert K., once, in his late seventies, was doing the roping during branding round-up, when his rope suddenly knotted on him, catching his first two fingers at the top knuckle, severing one and leaving the other joint swinging. Al ran to cut the rope to free him, and his father yelled "Tattoo that calf!" Only later, after the last two calves were branded, did old man Mitchell permit Al to fly him to the hospital.

"These cowboys," Sherrie says one night, "they're just a different breed. You'll see."

*   *   *

Each night, around 6:30, after what seems like the longest, hottest day I've ever lived, we drive the cattle slowly to a nearby waterhole to circle around them as they "mother up." Although the cows are kept in the corral during branding, they often lose track of their calves, what with all the excitement and new smells, and need this mothering-up time to reunite. Some of the cows are painfully full of milk by sunset, and tour the outskirts of the entire herd, lowing mournfully for their calves to come feed. Finally, each cow and calf get together, recognize an old familiar smell, and gently nurse.

At last, we load our horses onto the trailers, and head back to the ranch to scrub down and eat dinner. After a day that began at 4:30, the cowboys wash up, dress in clean clothes, and get a second wind. During branding and calving seasons, they work weekends, too, but other seasons they often spend their weekends partying in town, in Amarillo, or in nearby Tucumcari, returning Monday morning with hangovers and tomcat grins.

"Cowboys do everything hard," Sherrie says with a wink, as she gives me a sunset tour of the ranch. "They work hard, and they play hard."

A brief dust storm rises out of nowhere, scours the landscape, and subsides. I drive back to Rachel's and try to sleep, but, each time I close my eyes, I see, with all the clarity of a vision, cattle, sagebrush, and cowboys in the blinding sunlight. I blink hard, trying to erase the image that seems to have branded itself on my retinas, but cannot. So, regaled by the day's archetypes, I lie sleepless and enraptured for more than an hour.

3

The Tequesquite includes quite a few adobe buildings, deceptive-looking trailers (inside of which you may find a three-bedroom apartment, all paneled, carpeted, well appointed, and roomy), a plush guesthouse, a cookhouse, a bunkhouse, a corral, and sundry other homes and buildings. You don't know what surprise is until you drive what seems forever on the hot, dusty, out-in-the-middle-of-nowhere New Mexico prairie, open a door on a low, modest-looking adobe house, and find it furnished in French Provincial. I marvel at the decorative care that's been taken everywhere on the ranch, from the artwork on the walls to the quality of the linens and towels. An aquarium purls quietly in the Mitchells' house. And, in the bunkhouse, in addition to the ever-present artwork, there are electric blankets, a pool table, a color TV, a laundry room, a refrigerator stocked with cold drinks. This is no fly-by-night trail camp, but a ranch, a home, no way station through which cowboys drift. People live here. And though from time to time they must get depressed about the sorts of things people do get depressed about, I see few traces of it. Most people seem just too busy to be blue. And anyway there's a strong, high feeling of ribbing, gentle irony, and gusto. They are like the passengers on a long ocean voyage who, come better or worse, will be in one another's company for some time, and so had better do their best to keep it cheery.

The bunkhouse, in which three or four cowboys now live full-time, is like a dormitory whose best rooms one acquires by seniority. Nicely paneled, the building includes an assortment of single and double rooms, a laundry room and bath, and a sitting room, as well as a curious thin closet for hanging up chaps, hats, and gear. Twilight, you can't be certain the cowboys themselves aren't leaning there all in a row, their hats pulled down over their faces, their shirts hidden in the shadow, their forms unmistakably suggested by the lines going straight down from hats to chaps to boots. On the bulletin board, someone has tacked a photo of Ralph Ginzburg.

The modern cowboy carries a syringe instead of a six-shooter, wears bell-bottom jeans, dries his hair with a blow-gun, and watches color TV. But his chaps are as traditional as the mesas: plain, strong leather with large pockets to hold everything from veterinary tools to Chapstick.

"Is that Chap-stick, or *Sh*ap-stick?" I tease Sherrie Mitchell, who quips, "Around here, chaps are what you get *under* your shaps."

The best cowboy, by necessity, is a jack-of-all-trades: a veterinarian, a farrier, a horse trainer, a roper, a doctor, a reader of natural signs, a truck driver and mechanic, a cook, a barber, a leather smith, and a brawler. And, a century after the heyday of the Wild West, a cowboy's most important possession is still his boots. Pointy-toed, high-heeled (to hang better in the stirrup, and dig deeper into the dirt when flanking a calf), they usually have ornamental stitching, and are made of fine, well-treated leather. Often they have two finger-holes on either side at the top.

In this solar opus, where a western hat is all that sits between a man and sunstroke, everyone has a deep, mahogany tan—but only up to his forehead. Underneath his hatbrim, clear to the scalp, a cowboy's skin is pure white, as if it were a high-water mark. I remember that the Indian sign for the white man was two fingers held horizontally across the forehead—perhaps an allusion to the peculiar tan of the cowboy?

What a surprise to find they still carry and use ropes: to catch their mounts in the morning, to drag cows out of bogs, to catch calves for branding, to slap against the thigh when herding cattle, to climb rocky inclines, to kill rattlesnakes. But ropes I never hear referred to as *lassos* or *lariats,* just *ropes.* And these days they're made of strong, stiff nylon that bends easily into loops.

"One day, we killed five rattlers between here and that windmill," Scooter says.

"How?" I ask incredulously.

"With our ropes."

"Where do you aim for, the head?"

"Not especially," he says. "You can hit 'em anywhere. It's *how* you hit 'em that counts."

There are fence-riders and mill-riders (who check the windmills at each waterhole), but no longer the singing night-herders, who rode large slow circles around the herds, and exchanged a word or two as they intersected with a cowboy riding the other way, or sang to the herd to keep it calm.

When Al Mitchell's grandmother was alive, people from all over the valley came to the ranch for help or work, and, to a large extent, that is still true. The ranch has its own commissary and an ice house. Everything is bought by the crate and the gross. The emphasis is on being neighborly. If there's an orphanage in the area, the Mitchells, like the other ranchers, will assume responsibility for its support, stopping by with a bushelful of corn, or a few cows, or personal necessities. It's as if, out here where the land is so harsh that, to borrow a Werner Herzog title, it's "Everyman for Himself, and God Against All of Us," people just naturally feel protective of one another; it behooves them to be less harsh than the land.

"You have to be awfully self-sufficient to live like this," Sherrie explains. "A lot of people can't take it. Either they leave in a couple of months, or they stay forever. You see, out here all they have is each other, and if that won't do, there's no place to go."

One thing Al Mitchell is, is self-sufficient. The quintessential cowboy, strong, handsome, stoic, and possessed by a fine ironic sense of humor, he works even harder than his hired hands do, and often at the same jobs. When they're home from school (the oldest son is at Stanford, the others are at Deerfield Academy in Massachusetts), his boys are full-time cowboys, too. How good it must feel for a father and sons to ride out together and work together all day, instead of the father's fleeing to some abstraction called an "office," from which he returns, fatigued, at day's end. Each son is better-looking than the last, polite and unspoiled, yet very much in command. They are the bosses, and have a sense of helping out with the family business, just as any sons might, and, like their father, they work sunup to sundown in the wicked, soul-sapping heat.

Little Lynda, adorable in her dutch-girl haircut, isn't quite big enough yet to mount her horse, Dick, by herself, but can ride him like a pro already, knows how to herd cattle and help with calving. She remembers being held in her father's arms, in the saddle, even before she was old enough to walk. What a transformation: at night, she curls up in her nightgown to do a Snoopy needlepoint and, in the day, she rides out early to work the range.

Albert Mitchell is the son of a son of a son, but now there are three boys and, therefore, a choice for them. The youngest, Terry, hopes to be a veterinarian. The middle boy, Tom, who cowboys so well, wants to be a rancher. Scooter, the oldest son, is bright and sensitive: the future lawyer. Heading for law by way of engineering, he'll probably settle for land-law. And by the time he's a lawyer, the ranch may need one.

The modern ranch owner has trouble with environmentalists who want, for example, fences high enough for antelope to be able to slide under; trouble from the government, which wants to subsidize (but thereby control) the ranchers, suggesting hazard laws that cowboys often find unrealistic and unworkable; trouble from unions (in Hawaii, cowboys ride a forty-hour work week). I ask Al Mitchell jokingly one night if he and his boys ride forty-hour work weeks.

"Sure we do," he grins, "forty hours today, forty hours tomorrow. . . ."

Here, where the cowboy has evolved a highly specialized and efficient way of working, *standardization* is not a popular word. His chores may change wildly from day to day, depending on the season, the health of the animals, the weather. But, much more importantly, the cowboy *is* a "different breed," as Sherrie Mitchell claims. He might just as easily sell shoes or be a banker; he chooses this line of work because it means something to him. This grueling, lonely, rugged life appeals to him, permits him to define himself by its demanding criteria, as no easier job can. What's at stake is his personal freedom, and that he prizes more than money, hazard laws, or leisure.

"We *are* conservation," Al says as we drive back to the ranch one night. "We don't just fatten steers for market; we breed cattle. Ours is a long-range investment, and we have to care about healthy herds, enough water, good grazing land."

I ask then how he handles the ecologists who, from distant offices, urge him to adopt one land technique or another. And he explains that instead of arguing with them he just invites them to come see the ranch at work.

"They get the message fast," he says. "The rancher's boss is the land and the cattle, and that makes him one of the oldest ecologists."

With characteristic modesty, he doesn't mention the letter I found up on a bulletin board when I was ferreting through its splash of announcements one day. From a distance, it had seemed one of those endless edicts employers must issue concerning some wastage, new rule, or employee. But, closer, I discovered it to be a letter so plain-speaking and heartfelt it moved me. He was asking the ranch hands please not to kill any wild animals—coyotes, snakes, whatever—for their skins. He explained that if and when such killing became necessary, he would announce it, and they would be welcome to the skins; but, growing up in this country, he'd grown to love its animals, and would grieve if they weren't around for his grandchildren to enjoy. That's all: a simple, direct plea. And I remember how, late one afternoon, I'd seen Al, in the crazy uproar of branding, caked with sweat, and parched within an inch of his life, glance at the luscious bloom of a cactus just outside the corral, its magenta flowers gaudy and intense. In that swift, private moment, his face said everything about the beauty of the prairie.

I know the cowboy's stoic code of noncomplaint, his uncompromising yen for fair play, his work ethic, but not as much as I'd like to about his esthetics. Perhaps I am insulting this strong, tough-willed man to admire the tenderness of heart that animates him. I think not. Surely a man becomes a cowboy, in part, because the land enraptures him.

"How did you meet Al?" I ask Sherrie one night, and she tells me about the young rancher's son who decided, on their first meeting, that he would marry her, and so began wooing her with a stream of yellow roses. From there to the ranch it was a swift, if many-miled journey.

"You mean inside that tough hard-living cowboy exterior, there's a heart full of yellow roses?" I inquire, but it's a question Sherrie answers fully with a smile.

Albert Mitchell is the third Albert; his son, Scooter, the fourth Albert. There is a long tradition of their being here. And despite all the twentieth-century kudos (Al, among other things, is president of the New Mexico Cattlegrowers Association; his dad is in the Cowboy Hall of Fame; in the family, there are trustees and Congressmen, to mention but a scant few), they like ranching in the old-fashioned cowboy way. It agrees with their sense of tradition. Sherrie says, "We could do things the other way, but we like to do them the old way." And each day I watch the men rope, flank, and brand cows, or herd cattle over the cactus-strewn range, just as their fathers and grandfathers did. There are concessions to modern technology—a plane and a helicopter, butane burners to heat the branding irons, up-to-date veterinary care and nutrition, a small herd of pickup trucks—but the flavor is Old West and unmistakable. Secretly, I like it when one of the cowboys calls me "gringo," or Sherrie teases me with "tenderfoot," which I always thought referred to the unavoidable blisters a newcomer seems to raise. But no, a tenderfoot is a cow from a different country. And, out here, I am as rare as rain.

4

Come morning, in the cookhouse, I crack two eggs into a bowl, then drop them into the bubbly bacon grease, turning them occasionally with a spatula. Yawning, Mettie drops some eggs into a heavy black frying pan next to mine.

"Morning, cowboy," I greet him, as if he were a genre.

"Morning, M'am," he says, smiling mischievously. "Ready to flank some calves today?" He hands me a plate, onto which I slide the eggs and a pungent sausage patty.

"Sure am," I answer as resolutely as I can, and, indeed, I do feel game, curious, and willing, but hardly resolute. Perhaps I won't be strong-limbed enough to hold a struggling calf down, or strong-stomached enough to watch the castrating at such close hand. Perhaps the smell of the horn-singeing, like burning hair, and the calf's eyes rolling so white and translucent will turn all my muscles to water. Twice already, ropers (Tom and Scooter Mitchell) have had near-misses, been tangled in a flying line, or jumped clear of a falling horse, to be saved by Russell's timely slicing of the rope. Perhaps my bravado will endanger someone. What if I cause injury to one of these people I've grown so fond of? Camaraderie is a luxury a writer rarely has the privilege of feeling; so much of the work is done alone. But now, sitting at breakfast with the cowhands, I feel part of a team, and am grateful to know what that feeling is like. How wonderful it must be to grow up on a ranch whose well-being, in a real sense, you contribute to. A suburban girl may set the table, or help clean, or iron, but her chores are undisguisably trivial. She knows the whole shebang won't collapse in her absence, that no one's life depends on her. She may even sense, with a paling of her self-esteem, that her so-called chores are merely ruses to keep her busy and out of trouble. But on a ranch, as on a farm, everyone's work counts, adds up. Nothing is trivial; crops, animals, and people depend on you. No one is meaningless. The Mitchell children (ages ten to eighteen) are surprisingly mature and knowledgeable. They vary in temperament, but all seem willing to take responsibility for their own lives, in a way in which many, *most*, children are not. Nor could you ever accuse them of being solemn. Prankish and frisky, it's their balance of high spirits and self-composure that's so winning. And I think the reason is that the Mitchell children, like their parents and their cowboy big brothers, feel the kind of pride and dignity one does feel knowing that he is responsible for life: the lives of family and friends, the lives of horses and cattle. How rare and fine it must be to grow up feeling indisputably necessary.

Tom passes me a stack of buttered toast. We eat with none of the nervous, eye-of-the-tornado silence that characterized the first few breakfasts, when the only noise was a litany of requests for milk or jam, and the random clattering of cutlery. Now the boys pick up bacon with their fingers, and daub napkins to their mouths less obsessively. Little Britches tucks in a hearty breakfast without fuss. We chat idly. Someone warns of a patch of quicksand he found yesterday, into which a horse could disappear in a few minutes.

"Can you see that," someone else laughs, "walking back to the ranch, and trying to explain to the boss how it is you've lost *both* your horse *and* your saddle!"

We finish up quickly, and head down to the corral. Today I ride with Scooter again to drive cows from hinterland to waterhole. Scooter wears an ever-immaculate white plume in his western hat. I can't fathom, for the life of me, how it stays clean, what with all the ruckus and dirt of branding, in the thick of which Scooter always is. I josh him that perhaps it's a symbolic plume he wears, a feather of the psyche, that one day, triggered by heaven-knows-what thought, will suddenly go chartreuse or fuchsia.

On the distant horizon, we see a speck of black.

"There's a stray cow," I tell Scooter, pointing to the barely visible object.

"Cowboy," he corrects me.

And squinting, I can just make out a tiny nub on the black spot, a nub that signifies rider and mount.

As we trot the few cows we find toward a distant windmill, Lynda, engagingly chatty as ever, fills me in on the prairie flowers, locoweed, and sagebrush. Here and there, a three-foot-high cactus stands in bright-red bloom, each velvet flower shaped like a saki cup. The air is full of the high, reedy whine of crickets, like steel wires singing. And all around us, the mesas look stolen from some fairy tale: pale, sherbety ribbons of ocher, pink, and blue. Overhead, the sun burns white-hot already.

The other cowboys and the Boys Ranchers gather at the waterhole, riding in from all directions, like jets landing along different corridors. Already they've hooked up the green, portable corral in which we'll be branding today. Different quadrants of the ranch have their own "camps" (usually a shackhouse, a corral, a larder); but out here, rather than drive the cattle needlessly to such a camp, it's simpler to bring the corral with us.

R. J.'s skin looks so tanned and weathered that, for a moment, I think perhaps he is perplexed, but no, it's only the way certain of his wrinkles fall. Like a sorcerer to his apprentice, he shows me how to use the injection gun: how to balance the gun and bottle in one hand (you need the reach of a pianist) while coaxing the golden fluid into the chamber with the other, how to pierce the rubber gasket on one of the twenty or so bottles of chilled vitamin A, where to aim for on the calf's rump, when the syringe should be refilled, and how to deal with bubbles of trapped air.

Still, my first attempts are so shaky the needle doesn't even penetrate the calf's hide. To my embarrassment, I lose the needle somewhere, and check the calf carefully to make sure it's not in him. R. J. opens a pack of extra needles that looks like a perfect set of fountain-pen nibs. I let him install the needle tip, as he is better able, and then try again, this time jabbing fast and deep, squeezing the trigger, and withdrawing —all in as swift and as smooth a gesture as I can manage. It works, is easy in fact. And so, following R. J.'s lead, I move with him all around the corral, in a dusty *pas-de-deux*, as freshly flanked calves become ready for our ministrations. He counsels me to judge when the calf's least likely to kick its strong heels, before ramming my syringe solidly against the rump muscle, and firing the 3cc's of liquid health. R. J. inoculates the calves against blackleg while I vitaminize them, and though it sounds like simple work, one walks miles back and forth across that hot, cramped arena; one raises and lowers an arm a hundred times. One drinks quarts of lukewarm water without ever having to urinate; the tissues must constantly be cleansing themselves, replenishing their reservoirs, and sweating.

Russell sharpens his castrating knife on a palm-sized slab

of gray stone he carries in his chaps pocket. Here and there a cow pees unceremoniously, lifting its tail like a pumphandle. The air is 100° F, and feels it.

"Hang on there, cowboy, hang on!" Al yells to a struggling flanker, who's dragged a few yards down the corral.

Everyone works swiftly and with meticulous caution. Al is obsessive about safety, and his concern rubs off on his men, who seem to respond to danger instinctively and as a team. I hold the syringe close against my chaps, needle down, and keep an eye out for the hot irons and butane burners.

Scooter, his plume nearly white as the sun, lassoes a hefty calf and drags it out for the flankers. Across the corral, Tom does exactly the same. Instantly, ten people jump into action. Two other calves hit the dirt, kicking and bawling. Dust, sweat, and noise saturate the air.

Branding takes so much plain muscle power, and happens with such hullaballoo, that the cowboys' barrage of gentle ribbing that accompanies it comes as a merciful light relief. With the air thick as a dust storm, someone feigns a shoot-out with his syringe. Mettie teases R. J. that I should give him a dose of vitamin A.

"You know I've got to inject it in a muscle," I join in, "and, as you can see, R. J. doesn't have any."

Like the rest of the cowboys, R. J. is slim figured and tough willed. Once, even after breaking his pelvis, he was back roping, braced up, within a few months.

By lunchtime, I'm done for. My legs ache from all the squatting to give injections, and a little from standing up in the saddle at fast trots. We wash up at the waterhole, sharing it with a turtle and a fearless diamond-backed lizard. Jackrabbits spring out of low clumpy mesquite. I drink the well water greedily, let it splash over my wrists, wash my forehead and neck. Lunch is plentiful and savory, but I have to force myself to eat. *Hunger* is like an alien fever. I'm just too hot and tired. And the thought of something sweet, even Juanita and Porfia's dessert of lemon-blueberry cake, puts me off. Instead, I eat a little of the meat and vegetables, and drink a few cups of iced tea and water.

Sherrie brings a needle and thread (a request I'd had Al discreetly relay earlier over his truck's CB radio). And with that, Lynda and I mount up, and ride for the parched river-bed nearby, whose salty bottom will do nicely for a tailor shop, and latrine. I see nothing that resembles a riverbed, and then suddenly, over a rise, a large, carved channel leaps into view. Sitting at the top of the embankment, it occurs to me, oddly, that I've never climbed down a riverbank on horseback before. Lynda leads the way on her horse, Ranger; expertly she finds secure footing in the crumbly dirt, holds the saddle horn, and climbs down at a steep angle. I follow suit. There we dismount, and what a picture we must be! Sitting right out in the open, on a scorched riverbed patterned with salt-swirls and damp clay, on the New Mexican prairie, in my underwear and hat, while my horse stands ground-tethered nearby, I thread a needle and smile. What a vision. The sun feels warm as a tonic on my bare legs.

"Why don't you take off your hot chaps during lunch?" I ask back at camp. And, to a man, the cowboys look bewildered.

"Wouldn't feel right," they answer, "feel nekked without 'em."

I'm amazed to see how many men, on their feet all morning, eat standing up, using the truck hood as a table. Others snooze for a few minutes in the cabs of pickup trucks.

Another pair of girls rides out with the needle and thread. When they return, one of the Boys Ranchers does the same. It's been a hard morning for jeans, what with all the mounting, dismounting, fence-climbing, and flanking. Sherrie laments the nonstop stitching she must do just to keep the ranch clad and functioning.

* * *

By 1:00, lunch is over, and we start in again. Timidly, I ask Al if he'll let me flank and brand, and, to my surprise, he agrees, asking if I'd like to learn to castrate, too. I say no, my alarm thinly disguised, but add, "You know, rumor has it that's one thing we eastern girls don't need to learn."

Sherrie laughs generously, and confides she's heard sheep ranchers castrate with their mouths, which we both find repulsive in the extreme.

"If Al had been a sheep rancher," she says, "I'd never have married him."

"You sure as hell wouldn't have kissed him," I add needlessly.

But, truth told, Al would never let me try so delicate an operation. He does it deftly, swiftly, manipulating the testes out like two silver torpedoes, cutting them off and sealing the incision with a serrated tool, then disinfecting the wound. One clench by me at the wrong moment, one flinch, one pause to consider the quiddity of the beast, and there would be blood everywhere. I shudder and decline. But all afternoon, deadpan, the cowboys keep offering to let me try it. It's only when I turn my back that I sometimes hear a quiet chuckle.

One of the best cowboys, and the strongest, Mettie becomes my flanking partner, which I suspect is no easy assignment. In flanking, one man naturally leads; otherwise a 300-pound calf and spinning rope play havoc, and I am only too willing to do exactly what he tells me. Al asks Tom for a small calf, the way one might ask the local butcher for a pound of lean meat. And, with my heart beating like a pair of wings, Mettie and I dash after the roped calf, grab the noosed legs and toss it to the ground. Al literally moves my hands and legs to the right positions as, hopping over the taut rope (which Tom's horse holds steady), I flop down behind the calf's rump, untie the noose, and spread its legs at a sharp angle. All my limbs seem to rush hotly with adrenalin. Al moves the instep of my left foot until it sits squarely on the calf's upper thigh, as I grab the other struggling hoof with my hands. He instructs me to lean back. It's an odd posture, and takes all my weight to keep the calf's strong legs steady. The amount of sheer muscle needed to hold the calf is unthinkable. To relax, I puff my cheeks idly with air, a nervousness Mettie catches sight of, and we laugh. With energies at full stretch, small talk is hardly possible; and a laugh is your certain undoing. A calf leg squirms free and kicks up at my chin, which makes my hold on the other leg precarious. Any minute, the whole shebang will fall apart, I'm convinced, when Mettie leans over the calf's stomach, and helps me back into position.

Sweat running in muddy rivulets down my cheek, I lift the band of my hat just a crack to let the wind whistle under it. The corral is littered with bits of calf scrotum, dark hairy little talismans drying in the sun. Fence-tethered, or hobbled, the horses stand patiently, swishing their tails to drive off the ever-present flies. All this fracas is so familiar to them. It's only tenderfoots like me who jump at sudden movements or flinch at eerie moans.

Holding his knife high in the air, Al walks toward us, his boot sole worn and flapping (later, we'll have to fetch him another two pairs). He crouches nimbly, slits the bottom off the calf's scrotum with a swipe and, pressing just so, collects the testicles under the skin, then milks them out. The calf's eye spins again, but already much is happening around his head to distract him. A drop of blood flies up at me, catching me on the cheek. Al tosses the iridescent "oysters" into the bucket (held beach style by a little boy), and sprays the wound carefully.

Cranking my arms and legs, like a paper doll's, into the right position, Al shows me how to roll the calf over so its horn can be treated on the other side. Legs flail like two wild-cat boat rudders. We pin them, and again I rock all my weight back on my haunches, spread the calf legs stiff and straight, while Russell cauterizes the red caldera that was a horn.

Steers are dehorned like this to stop them from fighting with bulls, which can be dangerous for everybody, not least of all for the ranch hands. But the cows keep their horns, which curiously enough helps them to mother-up; it gives them a wider territorial span, and that means less crowding when at last they start searching in earnest for their misplaced calves.

Al cuts the ear, Scooter brands, R. J. and Tony give shots, while Don injects a pellet from what looks like a cap gun. And then we're finished. Mettie gives me the high sign to back off smartly, as he swings the calf around with a knack, and releases it. Dazed, it stands still for a moment, then trots nonchalantly into the holding pen, though moments before it had been wailing as if at the hands of the Inquisition.

In the truck sit three milk cans of lukewarm water, in each of which floats a Styrofoam cup or two. The first few days I'd drunk from them reluctantly, my eastern germ-training cautioning me loudly. But now I take a cup, like the other hands, dip it into the dusty water, and drink gratefully. So, too, from the water cans in the corral, though their liquid is warmer. Some of the men chew tobacco, like Mettie, to keep their throats wet, but most depend on the frequent swills of water.

I ask a cowboy what he does at night, knowing as I do that he's not allowed to drink, gamble, or carouse on the ranch. After dinner, he explains, he usually watches television, or listens to the radio, grateful, I suppose, that, unlike his cowboy predecessors, he doesn't have to ride "night herd" on the stock. By 9:30 or 10:00, he's asleep, since he knows he has to wake at 4:30 the next morning, well rested and ready for a taxing day.

"What ever happened to the romance of the cowboy?" I ask.

He gestures toward the corral, hot, dusty, loud, and full of achy muscles and dark ribbons of sweat.

"That's it. You're looking at it," he says, and dips his Styrofoam cup into the can of tepid water.

I watch the vapor from the branding trough shimmer like a mirage. Tom runs his used iron through the dirt, to free it of hair and blood before returning it to the fire. Al washes his hands and knife scrupulously, as I've seen him do so often in the course of the day. And I wonder if it isn't time for me to take the plunge. Certainly I'm much too tired to be nervous.

"Let's go," Al says, plucking a branding iron from its private inferno.

And, showing me how to hold the calf's snout down with my foot, he puts the iron into my grip, wraps his gloved hands around mine, and presses the iron into the jowl hair, sliding it smoothly. I watch the first stroke of the iron, hear the calf moaning, and recoil. Al takes my hand, forcing the iron down squarely into the fur to brand the rest of the **K** and, that quickly, we are done. But I'm shaken to within an inch of my soul, and wild with exhilaration.

Off and on, through this searing desert afternoon and the next, while calves kick up gritty squalls of dust, Mettie and I flank. Scooter and Al show me how to brand a few more times, but it still alarms me to think I might burn in too deeply or, worse, not deeply enough to scar properly. Soon my chaps are splattered with dirt, blood, and excrement; my eyelashes coated with a fine glaze of mud. I hurt brutally, and all over, but in no place I can localize. And something odd has begun to happen: light-years beyond the state we label *exhaustion*, I no longer feel hunger at all, not even after a grueling ten-hour day. I feel as if I've been driven to full stretch, and held there like a flanked calf, utterly used up. Never have I met anything so physically demanding; and, in some nearly mystical, inexplicable way, *it feels good*. For the first time in years, I feel completely, miraculously, alive.

But the woman in me feels dirty, sweaty, bloody, and hot. All she craves is cool, cleansing water, a good scrub-down, a little make-up, a dress, and a lively douse of Chanel. Such a process I begin at the waterhole on our drive back, by pouring water down my blouse, and then trying to cool the effervescent hot pulse at my wrists. Overhead, the windmill works hard in the light breeze, making an unforgettable snoring sound as it pumps. Days later, I will wake in the night to hear my husband snoring, and think for a moment that I am at a waterhole on the prairie. No, no, I will have to remind myself in the blackness, there are no mesas, it is not time to get dressed, you will not tumble into bed tonight feeling timeless and indestructible as the hills.

"Got a little bit of dirt on your nose," Sherrie laughs, when we arrive.

I am as caked with dirt as any African mud dancer, my hair ropy with it; even my legs feel gritty.

She asks if I'm sore or tired, and I tell her no, "intoxicated," then apologize for the poeticism.

"Occupational hazard," I wearily explain.

I *am* sore, tired, hot; but I am also intoxicated. Never have I worked so hard out of doors before, and the sheer physical excess is a tonic.

When I wash my face, the cloth comes away blackened. I drink tumbler after tumbler of ice water, then shower, and dress for dinner.

In the cookhouse kitchen, I find a neatly groomed Al Mitchell, filling his plate with hot dogs, beans, and fragrant vegetables. His eyes blink in a double take when he sees me.

"Hey, Mettie," he calls into the dining room, "come see your flanking partner in a dress!"

* * *

How can I be leaving, I wonder the next morning, as I drive my low-bellied Ford slowly along the main road to Highway 39, taking care not to lose any of the car's delicate underside in a pothole so far from fixability. *Leaving* is unthinkable after a week's stay. I feel too much at home in this desert caravansary, where the air hangs windless, like wash on a line, and the mind empties of all excess paraphernalia. Civilization doesn't exactly disappear; it just seems beside the point. Which day is which I began to forget early in my stay, when the sun generalized everything from toad to dust pellet. Daytime was bright hot, and evening dark hot. So clearly it is daytime as I crawl along the dirt road in a state of shock. How can I leave this ranch family I've grown so fond of in so short a stay?

Like a runaway, I pause at the main gate to fix the scene: sprawling flatlands the color of chamois broken by outcroppings of windmills, cactus, and cattle, pastel mesas striped like Jovian planets, and, at the far edge of vision, a tiny clutch of buildings only a native could define by its combination of angles. In one of the buildings, a little girl will still be asleep, in another will be the watch I left accidentally, and in another Juanita will just be starting a low fire under the morning's bacon grease.

An eagle's-eye view of the Tequesquite. *In the foreground*, the Mitchells' house, the guest house, and a garage; *in the background*, the cookhouse, bunkhouse, corrals and barns, foreman's house, and other buildings. *Off the picture*, the schoolhouse, Rachel's trailer, and various outlying homes and shelters.

Al Mitchell set for work.

Saddling up after breakfast.

Branding irons heating in their troughs.

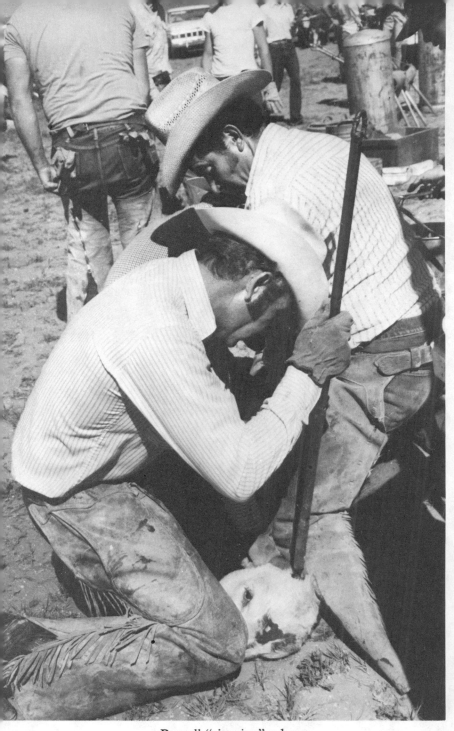

Russell "singeing" a horn.

Scooter roping a calf.

Hazing a heifer and calf into the right group.

Mettie and I have just flanked this calf, and are holding it ready for the branding team. The clenched teeth are because my shoulders feel dislocated.

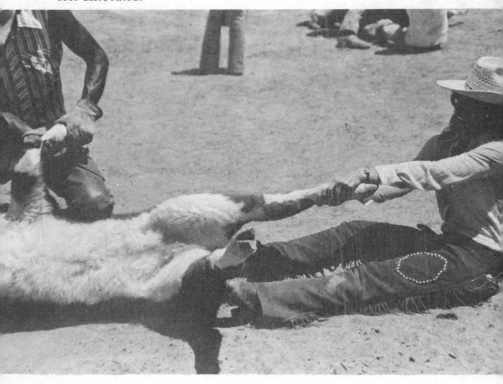

Don wrangling the day's horses in the eerie light before sunrise.

R. J. pausing for a drink of water. ". . . for a moment, I think perhaps he is perplexed, but no, it's only the way certain of his wrinkles fall."

The drinking cup which everybody uses.

Preface to Part II

In between bouts of packing for tomorrow's second trip to the ranch, I sip tea on the tree-ringed patio out back, and try to relax by watching quaking aspen leaves twinkle like coins against the blue sky. Twice today already I've skidded off the present and back a hundred years to a tinker living around the time when the Tequesquite was founded. I can just see him trekking across the prairie, his jingling pots and housewares shooting sparks of sunlight, see him flick idly at his horse's rump with a buggy whip, spit a dollop of tobacco juice into the road, and squint to pick out a landmark from the whitening glare of an anonymous sun: a sun abstract and unimpeachable. He wipes his forehead with a damp handkerchief, then rubs away the sweat beaded in his stubby beard, pockets the cloth, and finally, to let air cross his scalp, lifts the brim of a felt hat already clammy from early-morning heat. A tobacco-brown stain spreads halfway to the stain left by yesterday's long sweat.

"Yah!" he says, flicking his bay's rump with the whip, as

he turns up a dirt road to what may be a house in the distance. In his mind, nothing rattles but pots.

I check the fantasy, and retrieve the present: quaking aspen leaves, still spinning on their petioles, turn and turn about. On the yellow-rose bush (given to us by friends named "Busch"), a molar-sized beetle samples the sweetness of a tight, yellow bud. I'll have to do something about the bagworms in the mock hickories; but knowing how soon I'll be back at the Tequesquite acts like a potion, and again I drift away to the rolling prairie and mesas, cowboys putting their hats on two-handed, as if adjusting the sit of tight derbies, spurs glittery as sequins in the noon sun, Prince shying from a tiny shadow that represents heaven knows what terror to his alarm-ready brain.

Al Mitchell and I agreed, by phone, that he would meet me at Amarillo Airport this time, ferry me by car to a smaller landing strip nearby, and fly me to the ranch in his plane, only forty minutes away on a route straight as a yardstick, and then return with some of his family to Amarillo for a short stay, as if his whole vocation were nothing but finding his people, picking them up and putting them where they belong, a retriever rancher whose fatherhood I'm going to know even more closely over the next week or so.

PART II

Shipping Season

August / September

5

In July, the land had been parched and dusty, whereas now, only a month later, thanks to weeks of rain, the vista is green in all directions, the sagebrush lush as Arabian cushions scattered in a den of thieves, the stinkweed pungent, and the giant sunflowers rippling from one pasture to the next.

On the way to the airstrip (a lane of prairie kept cactus-free beside the hangar), Lynda and Rachel sing a current pop song, "Sunflower, Good Morning," and stop to pick a real sunflower through the truck window, giggling as they prune its petals: he-loves-me-he-loves-me-not. Two aging oranges sit on the dashboard. Al, Lynda, and Terry will fly back to Amarillo to join Sherrie and the other boys on a brief school-clothes shopping spree. Tom and Scooter, as if by previous arrangement, needed their wisdom teeth out simultaneously; now, at last, they are emerging from the hospital where, for such active boys, boredom numbs worse than anesthetic.

Rachel tugs a mentholated cigarette out of a soft pack, and

heads back toward headquarters, pausing at the crossroads to pick a sunflower through the window, again plucking its oracular petals. Like armies of bright-haired sibyls, sunflowers line the road on either side, as Rachel's green pickup truck bounces merrily over the dirt roads and cattle guards, its radio flooding the pastures with rock music as we pass.

Although technically all the pickup trucks are communal, each person has a favorite. Rachel's is green, for instance, Russell's white. Mettie has a new custom Ford that's rust and white (and a black one he bought, across whose back window runs a mural of mountains and sky). The Mitchells' giant rig, which they so kindly let me use during my stay, is entirely rust colored. There are golds and browns and other greens and whites, too, all so clean and gaily colored that, from afar, they look like Easter eggs nesting in the grass. At a glance, you know who's where. Mettie's black, satanic-looking truck, as we can see from quite a distance, is parked outside the bunkhouse, right next to Don's green one and Mike's white. Whether or not the Mitchell boys are home you can tell by how many and which rigs are out back. A Proustian memory invades my travel-weary senses. When I was little, I loved to play a boardgame called CLUE. Everyone got a different-colored marker and, in the course of the game, "Mr. Plum" would be "in the woodshed with Mr. Green," or "Miss White in the library with a gun and Miss Scarlet." That murder was the subject of the game, we hardly reckoned; what child could resist color-coded people, tiny metal weapons fit for leprechaun thugs, a house viewed from god's eye, all its rooms simultaneous? Mr. Plum, as even a five-year-old could plainly see, was ensconced in the kitchen where his color waited. People were as simple as they seemed.

Before dinner, I look down the road toward the cookhouse, and see Russell's white truck parked in front of his house; the girls, who have a truck of their own to drive to school in, still aren't home (perhaps it's Tina's basketball practice). Rachel's green pickup now stands outside the cookhouse where, probably, she's helping Adelina fix dinner. Lights burn in the bunkhouse windows. Sliding the glass door shut, I pad barefoot across the shag rug to the bathroom, and set my hair with electric rollers, then prowl around the schoolhouse, my new lodging, while they cook.

Schoolhouse is hardly the word to describe this pastel trailer furnished like a condominium apartment. Entering by the front door, you find a living room (couch, chairs, coffee table, bookcase) on your left, a modern kitchen (dishwasher, large fridge, table and chairs) on your right, dead ahead a laundry room with washer and dryer, and a hallway sharp as a T-square running left and right. Decisions. I snoop left, and find a music room or second bedroom; a master bedroom with king-size bed, walk-in closet and wrap-around-mirrored bathroom en suite. Down the other end of the hallway is an L-shaped schoolroom looking out onto a vest-pocket playground full of swings and jungle gyms. As a one-room schoolhouse, it straddles the centuries: blackboard, bulletin board, scissors, rulers, crayons, reference books, teacher's desk with a school bell on it, American flag and printed "Pledge of Allegiance," displays of students' essays and art projects; but also an electric typewriter, a stereo, all sorts of modern conveniences, and the newest textbooks. "Albert Academy," as it's called, is accredited, and, thanks to its necessarily small enrollment, the teaching style is as close to the tutorial ideal as you can get. This year, Lynda Mitchell will be a class of one. And like schoolgirls everywhere, she'll don her nicest school clothes in the morning, gather up her books and homework, and go to school. At recess, she'll play on the jungle gym and swings and, except for lunch, she'll not leave school till 3:00 in the afternoon, even though her house is only across the road, and *home* is all the land all the buildings lie on, almost as if they were merely rooms connected by dusty corridors.

I smile at the paneling and swanky decorative touches,

thinking of the urban schools I went to. But, come September, a schoolmarm will be living here full-time again, and things must be made as cozy for her as possible. It's a long way out for a young, single girl to live. I'm told the new teacher is from Sweet Briar, twenty-two years old, and pretty. Now she's just a smile in a photograph to most of the ranch, but by my next trip she'll be like a sister.

Clean clothes feel good. I stroll outside where the sun is just setting and, though I've never driven a truck before, hop into mine and drive down to dinner. Potholes teach me quickly what speed to use over the rain-snow-sun-sculpted road. The steel bars of the cattle guards, that can shake a fast-moving truck to smithereens, I remember graphically from my last trip, and drive slowly over them.

Only three cowboys live in the bunkhouse now the branding season's done: Mettie, Mike, and Don, although Navor Sr. (Mettie's uncle), Tony, and R. J. lend that mythic "hand" when it's needed. By the corral, Russell looks just as he did when I saw him last—sweat-stained, tanned, and sinfully handsome—as he grooms the young cream-colored horse his daughter Lace will show tomorrow at the county fair. Mike and I are the first to go in for dinner.

In the kitchen, a pretty, new cook smiles shyly from her fixings; Adelina of the sparkling glances is Mettie and Rachel's younger sister. With her husband, Juan, and their two-year-old daughter, Susie, she lives in an apartment connected to the cookhouse. Little Susie is shy, big eyed, and tiny featured, with just the right amount of bashfulness and dimples to be heart-stealing. She grabs her mother's pant-leg, and hides behind it, now and then peeking out with a grin. Everyone fusses over her, hugs and teases; and she adores being their babydoll.

Dinner is a mild chili served with thin, delicate tortillas which are fresh and warm, a bean salad, slivered potatoes, and, for dessert, iced spice cake. Mettie appears and, for a moment,

I can't fathom why he looks so changed; then I realize he's
trimmed his beard and moustache. The wildman's visage he's
traded in for the conquistador's. On his swarthy arms, covered
with freehand tattoos, veins rise stiffly, like dark ridges ribboned with coal. Don, pale haired and florid faced, still has
a white stripe running high across his forehead: the stigma
of a cowboy. He eats quietly, methodically, occasionally utter-
ing a spare word or two. Mike also has taken his usual seat,
two chairs down from Mettie, catty-corner to Don. Mettie's
English seems light-years more nimble than I recall its being;
but now I see it must not have been the language barrier that
ruled. This time around I'm a familiar.

Later, Rachel and Tina, Russell's older daughter, stop by
to sell a few raffle tickets and shoot the breeze. Like young
women anywhere, we swiftly cut the small talk and get straight
to gossip: all the ranch's intrigues. A few months short of
being twenty-one, Rachel is counting the days to her birthday
when, according to law at least, she can look after herself. As
her oldest male relative on the ranch, her brother Mettie is
protective as an Old-Testament god, threatens violence if he
catches her with any boy he doesn't approve of, is the watch-
dog of her honor, in an old world/*in loco parentis* sort of way,
even though their parents live only a few hours down the road.
It's a large, close family, the Gutierrez's. Rachel, Adelina,
Mettie, and Navor spend many days and evenings together—
by choice. And Juan and Mettie are as affectionate as brothers.
I learn, too, that all three cowboys have girlfriends they see
regularly, though the girls may live in Logan, Tucumcari,
Roy, or other nearby places. Sometimes the girls come to the
ranch, though no women are allowed in the bunkhouse—ever.
And I hear more about Mettie's nearly mythic list of brawls,
his quixotic valor with fists, knives, pool cues, or whatever
else comes to hand. Riled, he's a tough hombre, I gather; it's
a side of him I've not yet seen. But I can easily picture his

endless probations, regular as spring round-up, elemental, suited to him, as if it were a condition philosophically arrived at, an existential state, not a legal one. Other gossip I promise to keep under my hat, eastern or western, but it differs not a breath from the crushes, whims, and assignations, the habits, eccentricities, and squabbles one finds everywhere. The low-down is no lower on the ranch.

Intrigued as I am, what preoccupies me is not so much the gossip as what will happen tomorrow when I tug on my chaps. Later, in bed, I tremble sleeplessly for more than an hour until, at last, colors burst into the blackness like flak, and then carnival images begin to samba across the screen of my closed eyelids.

6

At five o'clock, after dreams of heat mirages and leggy
men, I wake, a few minutes before each of the alarms I've
staggered around the room. In turn, I plunge in their tiny
stems, then draw the curtains back for a glimpse of the early
morning mesas. But outside it's blue-black, windy, and star-
less. All I can see is my reflection in the glass: a puffy-lidded
raccoon with tousled hair. I run a tub, and pour some Murine
into my eyes, then bathe, dress quickly, put on my make-up,
set my hair with heat rollers, and paint my nails a satiny pink.
There's no time to try out the percolator and ground coffee
sitting behind a cupboard door, and making the room as fragrant as a rose garden or gin mill. *Tomorrow, five minutes
earlier*, I decree, and shut the schoolhouse door behind me.

Something large and living rises from its bed in front of the
pickup truck, its amber eyes gleaming. Then a sudden bark
calms me; it's only the German shepherd, Trampus. He keeps
his distance, but wags his whole body in excitement, flexes

like a spring, bucks stiff-legged as any bronco, minces and fawns.

"You don't even know me!" I whisper, nonplussed by the anonymity of his devotion, but can't resist patting him a few times over, as he wishes. Are all dogs extroverts? I suppose they are. Like a porpoise daring the bow of a ship, Trampus runs in front of the bumper all the drive to the cookhouse. Twice he sinks from view and, in alarm, I brake hard, then let my heart and truck proceed with a sigh when he bobs up again, tail wagging.

Already a pale streak of fire, rising over the horizon, makes the brick-red corrals and holding pens just visible. Purple clouds drift thinly across the sky, and in the east Venus is as loud as a thunderclap.

On a wrangling horse, Mettie ambles out of the corral.

"I'm late," he says, and I insist that I am late, too. How surprised I am to see him out of his western garb, looking so man-in-the-street-like, so collegiate in clean jeans and fresh shirt.

"*¿Donde está el caballero?*" I ask. "*Los chaparejos y el sombrero.* You left the cowboy hanging in your closet."

He laughs, and rides out to wrangle the herd of horses, while I stroll into the cookhouse for breakfast.

At exactly six o'clock, the gloom lifts and on the breeze I can hear Mettie's whoops and hollers, as he rounds up the quarter horses grazing in the dry creekbed, and drives them back to the corral. A line of sooty clouds looks like a fortress in the sky. The silence is almost a burden, so pure is it; and yet I've also been hearing the voices of countless insects and birds, whistling, singing, rasping tiny fugues, for hours (if indeed they ever sleep): flute runs, hinges slowly creaking, sandblocks and kazoos, reedy whines, plummet sounds, tissue paper being riffled. What could be a birdcall in the distance again is Mettie. Lace's palomino trots nervously around the corral.

By seven we are under way, hauling our horses behind us. It's a long drive by truck to the pasture where Mettie works today. On the radio, which the cowboys keep on constantly, the usual rock and country-western singers croon about lost loves or found loves or cowboying. One local favorite is a jaunty manifesto called "I Am a Redneck." The ranch people know all the singers and songs better than they do the names of local flora. Droves of records and tapes lie in every building, and long hours spent driving from one part of the ranch to the next are both enlivened and neutralized by a stream of music.

Our job in this far pasture is to check the 200-or-so cows for pinkeye and other ailments. But the herd is spread out; so we leave the pickup truck outside the pasture fence (lest a stray cow scratch it with an eager horn), unload our horses, check the girths, have a final swig of water, and ride off. Although it's hard keeping a camera securely bound to the saddle horn—no wedge, knot, loop, or strap will do for very long—I can't resist taking the extra set of eyes with me, the permanent eyes that see all and feel nothing. We break into an easy lope, and the ride is as comfortable as sitting on a porch glider on a summer evening in, say, Nebraska. But the western stirrups arch my ankles sharply, and a low-voltage ache begins that will only quit finally a few days later. Mettie has trained his palomino, Nugget, to lope as slowly as other horses trot, to roll its hips in a quiet, easy cadence that makes the long day in the saddle less tiring for both of them. Speaking gently to him with hands and legs, I try to chivvy Prince into the same cradle gait; and, given no option, he does rock for a few yards in that drifting-along, tranquilizing half-lope. But it bothers him; he shakes his head as if holding in a sneeze, and gratefully lengthens into a pace he prefers.

For most cowboys, a horse is just a different kind of truck. But Mettie really loves horses, responds to them esthetically, and trains them well. When he was little, his dad put him up on broncos; and, at first, he broke horses for the Mitchells. He tailors those in his remuda* to his special needs or whims, preferring palominos with what he calls "action," flashy, high-spirited ones with a touch of mayhem just under the surface. I notice that, doing whatever work, he takes time to discipline a quarrelsome or lazy horse on the spot. If it lets the rope slacken when it's supposed to be holding a cow on a taut line, if it shies from a lasso dragging behind it, if it refuses to sidle up to a windmill or waterhole, if it spooks excessively at a shadow or bird—Mettie stops, corrects the horse, then continues. Sometimes I see him working a rope as he rides, passing it around and around a spooky horse until the terror of that thin, flying circle becomes commonplace, and the horse settles down to an unperturbed jog.

We talk for hours, casually, as we ride, and I try to explain that my name, Diana, means the goddess of the moon, *la encantada de la luna*. But *encantada* is not a familiar word to him.

"*Como un dios, pero una mujer,*" I struggle in Spanish.

"*¿Dios de cielo?*" he asks. God of the heavens?

"No, no, *una diosa quien* controls *la luna*." A woman-god who controls the moon.

Suddenly he eyes me as if I were a savage worshipper of a very kinky sort.

"You believe that a woman controls the moon?!" My self-taught Spanish gives me no leeway.

"Well, actually it's a myth. . . ."

"What's a *myth*?" he asks blankly.

And for a moment I feel like a cow in a mazy corral, wondering which avenue will lead me home. Mettie is wickedly clever, bilingually witty, but completely self-educated, and myth may not be something he's consciously aware of. Should I tell him that in these myths a lot of lewd people live in the

---

* Extra saddle horses; from the Spanish, *remuda,* for "remount."

heavens and cause trouble for people on earth? I decide not to complicate matters. Instead I explain that in an old story, a story very much like a novel, Diana, who is also a huntress, has a bow and arrow with which she kills any man who makes a pass at her. This he follows only too well.

"She was a mean lady," he says in surprisingly idiomatic English.

"Very."

"And your mother named you after this mean lady?" He's incredulous.

"Yes, but I don't think she felt I had to live up to my name."

He shakes his head and grins. Obviously, he hasn't gotten over the fact that I believe there is a woman who controls the moon.

His name, he says, means nothing at all, is just a tag. Gutierrez, of course, is a common surname; offhand, I can think of three classic Gutierrezes: the Uruguayan poet Amador Gutierrez, the Guiterrez whom T. S. Eliot describes in the closing stanza of "Animula" as being "avid of speed and power," and the sadistic jailer Gutierrez in Edward Abbey's sonorously written novel *The Brave Cowboy*. There must be thousands. But Merejildo (whose abridged "Mere" we pronounce "Mettie") is far rarer. I make a mental note to pry into its origins when I return to Ithaca.

The recent launch of the spacecraft *Voyager*, complete with recorded music and spoken good wishes, he missed only because the bunkhouse TV was on the blink. Most of the spaceshots the cowboys see in glowing, if not quite Martian, color. Asked if he'd like a ride on the space shuttle, he shudders.

"Too dangerous."

As if what he did every day *weren't* dangerous. But perhaps a familiar danger is preferable to an unfamiliar one.

"Do you think there's life on other planets, *vida sobre las otras planetas?*" I ask, wondering indeed how much he knows about principles of astronomy. I'm surprised to discover how pervasive, how intrusive television is. He hears that scientists think there may be life on Mars, though he himself is unpersuaded.

"And elsewhere in the solar system?" The question doesn't faze him, but he thinks not.

I tell him that, myself, I believe there is life elsewhere, though perhaps at a considerable distance, perhaps in a far corner of our galaxy, and almost certainly in a curious form. But it would be nice to think that right now, on a planet circling a distant star, two beings may be riding on a prairie just like this one. The mirrored notion amuses us, each for different reasons.

I've no idea how cowboys manage as easily as they do to recognize tiny shapes at long distances. Looking for sick cows, Mettie can tell instantly if one is ailing, and at a distance at which all cows look the same to me. Mettie checks them carefully, one by one, keeping a mental note of which are lame, which need doctoring. He knows all their brambly hideouts, and checks derelict buildings for bovine tenants.

Thanks to the recent rains, there's mud in the creek and even a little water. Elsewhere, the waterholes are full, some of them deep enough to swim in. I suppose everyone is used to the heat, but I'd be tempted to spend my summer noons frolicking in the cool, dark waters, then drying off on the bank, under the sauna-sun. Though Mettie grew up on a peninsula, he doesn't swim, which must make wire-stringing over flood-torn creeks unnerving at times, and, at others, frightful.

Through the blistering morning, we chat idly about everything from drugs to scuba-diving (mine; he's curious). He sweeps an arm wide to embrace 180° of sage, mesquite, and cactus.

"On the bottom of the ocean," he says, "it looks like this?"

He could not be righter, and I recall my first impression of the daylight prairie: driving under blue waters on the ocean floor.

"Exactly!" Sandy and kelp strewn, with coral looking like bleached tree cacti, and here and there a tiny clump of color. Only the birds piercing the blue are fish.

Mettie's talk is utterly idiomatic: idiomatic Spanish and idiomatic English. And it's not unusual to hear him say things like "I can't hack it," and not understand words like *chaos* or *slang* in either language. His needs never require such expressions. In fact, many of the Spanish loan words English abounds with are as foreign to him as *encantada* was. *Brio, bravura, bravado*: he's never heard of them. *Macho*, of course, he knows the anglicized meaning of ("like a big-daddy stud"), though for him, as for most Spanish speakers, the word simply means masculine, and not excessively so.

"How do you say a man is strong?" I ask.

"*Fuerte.*"

"And if he is brave?"

"*Fuerte.*"

"And if he is full of life and zest?"

"*Fuerte.*"

"And if he is very sexy and masculine?"

"*Fuerte*. And to say someone is pretty—on the ranch we mostly say '*bonito.*' "

"Never *guapo*, or *lindo*?"

"*You* can," he says, "but we don't."

As isolated as the ranch is, it has developed its own lingo. *Spanglés* was never spoken more intently.

Jogging along the creekbed and up through some brambles, I notice that his worn, sienna-brown chaps are torn at the pocket. He pulls the flap up to show me the original color: brilliant scarlet. When he lets the flap fall, the heart-colored suede disappears. What a strange bright secret. Like the frilly underwear I put on under the blue jeans and chaps every morning.

"Last time I was here, I didn't hear anyone cursing, not even during branding! You didn't curse because of me, right?"

He confesses that it's true, adding that most of the men curse in Spanish anyway.

"How about teaching me to curse like a *vaquero*?" I ask gamely.

Shaking his head with a grin, he complies. "Tell me what you want to know."

I decide on the basics. "When you're furiously mad at someone, what do you call him?"

Mettie looks tentative. Men don't curse in front of respectable women in these parts. "You mean a very rank word?"

"The rankest."

He teaches me a handful of furious obscenities, phoneme by phoneme, which I commit to memory. It's like a scene out of a Berlitz school for hooligans. Cursing coolly in a foreign language I find a snap, since all the words sound equally alien; I might as easily be saying "swimming pool" or "cardsharp." I trade him a few choice words in German, noting how the Germans form compound words, how English, Spanish, and German have similar Indo-European roots, and other equally abstruse word things. Mettie follows the linguistics with interest and, later when I'm inspecting one of his work gloves, remembers with some amusement that Germans call it a "hand shoe."

Ranch humor is slapstick; there is a kind of repartee, but it's rarely verbal. Throughout the morning's ride, for example, each of us tries to catch the other off-guard, then spur or slap the other's horse into a rider-startling gallop. Now, while I rest my feet out of the stirrups, Mettie does catch me off-guard, so much so that it even surprises him, as Prince flies out from under me, and I topple around in the saddle, just short of a backward roll.

"I was nearly *patas arriba!*" I cry, "all twisted up."

No, he explains, *patas arriba*, which indeed I almost was, is a little different. When, as I'd told him earlier, I crossed the Atlantic in a jumbo jet and slept with my feet up the side of the wall—*that* was *patas arriba*, literally with my "hooves in the air."

When Mettie's not looking, I yank briskly on his back cinch, pulling it up tight like a bucking strap. Nugget ripples for a second, but Mettie quiets him, then sends him into a vaudeville shuffle on purpose.

"All your horses are palominos?" I ask, as he pats Nugget's lustrous neck. "You like blondes, huh?"

"Only horses," he answers diplomatically. "At breakfast, my grandfather spoke to you in Spanish; he thought you were a Spanish girl."

"You mean he thought I was a stuck-up Spanish girl for not answering."

What I don't tell Mettie is how last trip, stopping for breakfast in a roadside diner, I'd received unmistakable glares from some of its patrons. Above the grill, a sign read: WE RESERVE THE RIGHT TO REFUSE SERVICE TO ANYONE. Looking as dark and Mediterranean as I do, I've passed for everything from Turkish to Puerto Rican. Spanish I'm not, but a blend of Russian, Polish, and Austrian. Still, my ancestors didn't get from Palestine to Eastern Europe on magic carpets; somewhere somebody must have dawdled with a Spaniard or an Italian.

I ask Mettie if he knows of any cowboys who are gay. Again he shakes his head and grins. I ask some strange questions, but he understands why I might wonder about men whose work isolates them, prison or Army style. No, he insists, not the men he knows; self-image forbids it.

"You're so far from towns. And what did the cowboys do before, when there weren't any cars?"

"Rode horseback. Walked."

"But the distances were great!"

"So was the need."

Mettie has a girlfriend in Logan he visits most evenings and appears to be serious about. Could it be that, at twenty-eight, he's finally settling down? The ranch wonders, and holds its breath.

"Will you marry your girlfriend in Logan?" I ask, apropos of nothing.

He shrugs his shoulders, looks unhurried as the empty sky. "Depends on the weather."

Mid-morning, Mettie asks, "What time is it, about 10:18?"

I look at my watch: exactly 10:18, not a minute earlier or later. I'm stunned.

"How on earth do you do that?"

"Shadow of the horse." He shows me. "When the shadow is dead in front, it's lunchtime. So you judge how it is one side or the other."

A horse for a sundial. I can't even tell what *part* of the day I'm in.

After checking another pasture, we head back the long drive to headquarters, unload the horses, and unsaddle them in the corral. Without thinking, I take off Prince's bridle, then unlatch his girth and try to pull the saddle off, though, too late, I see the back girth is still tightly fastened. In that second, Prince dashes off at a gallop, the saddle trapped and hanging under his stomach.

"Aiyii," I moan, *"Estoy MUY estúpido."*

"Estúpida," Mettie corrects me, controlling his temper.

Meanwhile, Prince makes a circuit of the corrals, kicking and bucking violently, until finally Mettie corners him and releases the saddle whose leathers, miraculously, have survived all but a small rip. I apologize deeply, and feel foolish. An English saddle has only one girth and, in my fatigue, I'd forgotten the western saddle's double rigging.

"*Muy estúpida*," I mumble, my grammar, small consolation though it is, finally correct.

Lunch is an instant replay of last night's stew meat (this time in a savory sauce), potatoes, vegetable salad, and chili. Today there's a hot sauce, which Mettie offers me as "salad dressing." I spoon some on the chili, like the cowboys do, take a mouthful, and belch a dragon's flame of fire.

"I didn't do anything," Mettie says mischievously, as I disembowel him with a look. "I didn't do anything; Miguel told you to try it."

"I'm going to fix you, *vaquero*," I swear as my eyes tear hard from the red peppers, "it may take me all week to figure how, but I'm going to fix you." My tongue feels scoured by steel wool; my sinuses ache. Mettie ladles another few spoons of hot sauce onto his chili, now coated with enough red pepper to kill a rat, and calmly eats.

After lunch and an hour's siesta, we get ready to truck out with Juan, to rope sick animals and haul them back for treatment. At the corral, Mettie hands me Prince's bridle, says, "Okay, go get Prince," and, taking a rope from its hook near the tackroom door, he briskly lassoes a white-socked palomino. I spread the bridle and royal-blue noseband in my hands, walk professionally into the far corral, and bridle the wrong horse. Prince is the other chestnut, the one with the clean, distinctive star on his face.

"Aiyyii," I sigh, and go for Prince who, like many of the horses, is plenty savvy about not being caught. He darts behind an oozy, unwelcoming mud bog which he finds cool and refreshing in the summer, but has learned humans are reluctant to cross. Mettie, on horseback by now, drives him into a smaller corral. And there I finally cut Prince to a halt by dogging his sudden turns the way *he* dogs a steer's. At some

crucial moment, signaled by who knows what, all the counterturns, turns, counterturns stop, and Prince gives up. I slide
on the blue noseband, which usually has a snug rope-rein
attached to it—something to steer with if, far from the ranch,
the bridle should break—then speak softly as I try to slip
the bridle on. Prince jerks his head, and starts to back away.
"There, there," I murmur, jamming my thumb inside his
cheek just behind the teeth, which forces his mouth open to
receive the bit. I lift the headstall over his ears and buckle the
throatlatch. Gripping the bit, he rolls it around his mouth a
little and then, apparently finding the best place for it, stands
calmly. "Easy, fella." I pass the reins once through a hitching ring mortared to the stone wall, but know Prince is un-
likely to be there when I return. So, in a flash, I raid the tackroom for blanket and saddle, which I leave on the ground
by the door while I catch Prince and tether him to the hitching ring again. The striped blanket I drag down his withers
and onto his back, in the direction the hair grows, so it won't
chafe. But the saddle is almost too heavy to lift; its blockish
stirrups keep slapping me in the face as I take a deep breath
and, like a weight lifter trying to press a barbell, I jerk the
saddle to shoulder level, then swing it onto the horse. Juan
has not stopped smiling since we entered the corral, and now
struggles to hold in a laugh. I release the trapped stirrup
leathers and cinch from under the saddle, then, returning to
the correct side, reach under the belly for the dangling cinch,
lace it tight, and hook it on a metal tongue. Mettie slouches
against the fence, where he, two horses, Juan, and the trailer
all wait for my slowpoking to conclude.

Already sweat trickles down my cheeks. The pale fire of
the sun is singeing. I lead Prince out of the corral, twist his
reins, toss them around his neck a few times, and load him
onto the truck.

"*La pálida lumbre del sol está intensa,*" I say under my

breath, as I mop the sweat from my neck. Now I know why Sherrie and Lynda have short hair.

"*No comprendo*," Mettie says, overhearing me. "*Qué es eso?*" What's that?

"Ah. A poeticism in Spanish, probably. *Lo siento, acaso unas palabras poéticas. No importa.*"

Juan, who speaks almost no English, mimes to me that, for him, a *lumbre* is a very small sun, a spark. *Fuego* is his fire. The piffling Spanish I've committed so scrupulously to memory is book-Spanish gleaned from a dictionary and *Spanish in Twenty Easy Lessons*. Some of the words are familiar to Juan, who is from Mexico. But New Mexico Spanish is an outpost language, the lingo of a people between cultures, and therefore probably closest to Renaissance Spanish (spoken by the first Spanish immigrants and, over the years, contaminated wildly by English, but very little by modern Spanish). A linguist's delight, but a student's heartache. The bilingual slang reminds me of Vladimir Nabokov's erotic spree, *Ada*, in which he puns in three languages—and glosses none of them.

As we hop into the truck and head out for the far pasture, Mettie clicks on the radio with the habitual ease of an addict. Tanya Tucker wails a bluesy love song, "You are so beautiful . . . to meeee. . . ." And the sunflowers, at eye level, race past each window.

"Go ahead, tell him what I teach you to say," Mettie urges me. Phonetically, I stumble through a few graphic expressions. With each utterance, Juan smiles broader and blushes deeper. He can't believe Mettie's taught me such filth.

"How do I say, 'don't tell anyone,' in Spanish?" I ask.

"*No diga a nadie.*" Mettie repeats it slowly for my anglicized ears: "*No . . . diga . . . a . . . nad-i-e.*"

I parrot it a few times, then turn to Juan, as if to relate a bit of news, "*No diga a nadie.*" Hearing the expression a dozen times in a couple of minutes, he starts to laugh.

"*Bueno,*" he says. Okay.

Juan is handsome: slender, dark, and moustachioed. Very shy and sweet, though at home he's the undisputed lord and master. At twenty-five, he cowboys well and quietly, ropes and herds as if he'd been at it lifelong. And few things are more exciting than watching him fly after a panicky steer and work it, second-guess it, back into the herd. Adelina he met when she was only thirteen, fell in love with her, and wanted to marry. Now, four years later, though they have a two-year-old daughter who is an American citizen, money in the bank, steady work on a reputable ranch, and bosses who vouch for them, still Juan has trouble being legitimized by the US government. Meanwhile, Adelina cooks up snazzy meals (all the cowboys are heavier than when I last saw them), and Juan cowboys with his brother-in-law, Mettie, each day, then returns home to a quiet evening with Adelina and little Susie.

At each pasture fence, Juan leaps out of the pickup truck, unlashes the barbed-wire gate with a gloved hand, and closes it up again after the truck passes through. Finally we reach the pasture where, in the morning, Mettie saw a few lame cows. This time we drive the truck deep into the pasture, and untrailer our horses by a waterhole. On horseback, we inspect the grazing herd. Even I can tell which cows are limping, but Mettie needs to judge which ones might be ailing. He nods toward a gimpy cow, unties one of the rawhide ribbons around his rope, and that quickly he and Juan are off at full speed. Mettie swings the rope in large circles and flings it; with the other hand, he dallies the loose end round the saddle horn. This trick I've seen before in the branding corral, but what a thrill to see roping out in the open! Juan leaps off his bay, and runs to help catch the roped cow. Off comes the lasso from its legs, and on goes a halter made *ad hoc* from a spare rope. They lead the cow back to the truck without trouble, but it refuses stubbornly, obtusely, and loudly under any condition whatsoever to set foot in the trailer. Mettie feeds the halter

line through one of the bars, and pulls with all his might
while Juan, shoulder to the cow's rump, cranks the tail and
pushes simultaneously. Hoping to startle the cow, I yell and
whoop. Nothing seems to work. Mettie says something fast
in Spanish. And, sweating profusely, Juan agrees. For a moment, they rest, then marshal their energies again. Tempers
rise as fatigue sets in, and the cow seems, if anything, now
anchored to the ground. The two men are straining hard, and
I feel bad for them, but how beautiful they look: like a single
muscle flexing and relaxing in the heat, flexing and relaxing.
Mettie says something else fast in Spanish. Though he knows
I don't know the language, he's taking no chances. Teaching
me to curse has nothing to do with the fact that a man doesn't
curse in front of a lady. He takes a break to pour a capful of
water from the pickup's canteen. I have some, too, though I've
not earned it.

"¿Más?" he asks.

"No, bastante. . . ."

"No, no bastante," he instructs me, "decimos 'suficiente.' "
We say sufficient. He tosses the cup's remaining drop of water
into the dirt.

I want to kill the author of Spanish in Twenty Easy Lessons.

Back to work, our dusty mouths refreshed. To see Juan and
Mettie size up the situation from a distance, like two artisans
inspecting the angle of a cathedral arch, I laugh quietly. We
have a problem.

"Okay, vamos," Mettie says, "you push the tail." And so I
do, as he and Juan literally lift the half-ton cow into the
trailer, one leg at a time. It's grueling work, and this is only
the first cow. In she goes, finally, bawling all the way. How
could she know what ministrations await her. Juan takes his
cap off and sets it back on his head. Mettie re-coils his rope.
Without complaint, they mount up and ride after the next
cow.

Why, I don't know, but the waterhole just isn't pumping

properly. The windmill's blades twirl in the light breeze, but no water gushes—in a landscape so dry water-questing becomes a mania. We must drive the herd to another mill in the distance.

"Thatta way," Mettie waves vaguely, as he rides off to steer the front of the herd. But I've no idea where we are to begin with, let alone where the next waterhole is.

"You can see it?" I ask Juan.

Yes, he can see it in the distance, and points to something that is there for him, but not for me. I squint hard against the glare of the afternoon sun, and *try* to see it: a tower, a fleck, a shadow on the horizon. Nothing. Yard after yard, I blindly group the herd, letting Juan lead the way. Finally, over a rise, a bit of scaffolding stands out against a mesa. Now I know where to move the cows.

"Gitta-long! Gitta-long!" I yell with gusto.

Juan whistles, yelps, calls *"Muévete!"* (Move yourself!) or *"Vamos!"* (Let's go!), *"Vamos, vacas!"*

Close to the windmill, Mettie stops to let the cows drift in by themselves. A scintillation in the dust catches his eye; jumping down, he pushes aside a clump of mesquite, then mounts up and lopes toward us. In his hand is a rusty, well-made penknife that a summer cowboy, Pierre, lost a month before. He rubs it briskly on his jeans, and puts it in his pocket, pleased by the long-shot of finding it at all in these acres upon acres of ranch. Juan and Mettie exchange spark-like glances, and then they are off at the fastest clip I've ever seen outside a race track. Prince doesn't wait for a second bidding to do the same, although to catch up with them he'd need to be a nuclear-powered Pegasus. I get high from this free gallop, thrill to it, pant hard out of exhilaration, as Prince races the short distance to the truck. Warm winds whip by like a sirocco's, and the saddle horn rolls back and forth at such speed my mind skids into a dream of camel-riding. When the wind pulls on my hatbrim, I could as easily be wearing a *djellib* as I sprint over the sand dunes in some sheik's cavalry. I'm sure Mettie and Juan have no notion what possesses me as, dropping low and limp in the saddle, I let Prince thunder the last few yards to the truck. Upright again, and recovered, I pull Prince in gently, and pat his sleek neck.

"Such a good *caballo*," I coo, stroking his chest with a loving hand, "such a sweet *caballo*." I run my hand down his mane and straighten his forelock, a few wisps of which cling to the headband, then twist the reins round his neck, and load him onto the trailer.

On the radio, "Sunflower, Good Morning" is followed by a down-home, chatty song by Johnny Cash, then an upbeat one about being thrown over for a fast-spender, one in which a twangy woman bemoans her husband's cooling ardor, and finally a man singing about how he's "easy, like Sunday morning." I feel as if I've just tramped through six lives in fifteen minutes.

"Do you dance?" I ask Mettie over the wail of a mournful ballad.

Although it's popular locally, he doesn't particularly enjoy barn-dancing. But once, he says smiling, he learned to do the "bump" at a discotheque he went to with his brother in Amarillo.

I pause to conjure up such a picture: this cowboy sitting beside me in chaps, hat, western boots, and work gloves, doing the "bump" to Charlie Pride while a strobe light flickers.

"Movies?"

Occasionally he does go to them, his preference being, naturally, for westerns.

"But you're a cowboy. Why would you want to see cowboys in the movies?" I ask, puzzled.

"Oh, they give me ideas what to do when I come back," he laughs. "Shoot 'em up."

Like all professionals, the cowboy fantasizes being supreme at his job, legendary, and Mettie is no exception. So he reads westerns and watches Gary Cooper, John Wayne, and Clint Eastwood. The closest theater is in Tucumcari, a few hours away, but a colossal ranch antenna brings in movies by the score.

" 'Bout 4:20?" Mettie asks Juan. Juan tilts the face of his watch toward us. It's 4:18.

"How do you do that?" I ask redundantly.

"Sun," Mettie shrugs, and pulls up to the next pasture gate, where Juan jumps out and wrenches the barbed wire back again, waits for us to pass, and refastens it.

"Stomach, too," he adds, "when I get hungry it's mealtime."

Sundials and stomachs. I explain that in my work I'm rarely outside for long, certainly never at the same time for the same spell every day, that I eat breakfast and lunch at irregular hours, and that some days I couldn't tell you if it was 11 A.M. or 4 P.M. It's an odd life, he thinks, just sitting at a desk, putting one word after another, and sometimes talking with students about putting one word instead of another, indoors. He's right; most days it's a dull, lonely, and splintered life, which is why I often need to wallow in being physical, in riding herd and branding, in just living. I do have the good fortune to be able to take my work with me whenever I go skylarking, can scuba-dive or fly or cowboy or ski *and write about it*, so I never have to feel I'm shirking my poetic duties.

"You like going a lot of places, seeing a lot of things?" he asks.

"Yes, I'm crazy about life," I answer too briefly, "all of it," and add, lest he misunderstand, "oh, I don't mean that I'm reckless or foolhardy, just curious. But with me curiosity is like a religion."

He folds a plug of chewing tobacco into his cheek, and offers me a chew from the fragrant pouch. I'm tempted, but resist for the moment. Juan, I notice, has begun to earnestly watch the sunflowers rolling their saffron heads in the light breeze. I see them reflected in his brown eyes, but no, it's only a glint of sun.

7

One morning, after the cowboys ride out in pairs and threes to round up cows from far-flung pastures, Al and I drive down a sunflower-banked road to the airstrip, where an aluminum dome houses a glossy new helicopter. Inside the hangar are also welding tools, spare parts, and other flight-related items; and, behind the hangar, a cement slab, that looks like a porch, used for take-offs and landings. Solid footing. The night before Al's due back in plane or helicopter, Rachel leaves a pickup truck on the slab, like a metal offering, out of the mud and dust, to await his arrival. Occasionally, he flies in a mechanic from Amarillo to service the helicopter in the hangar's own workshop. And last summer a private pilot gave each of the Mitchell boys daily flying lessons. The modern rancher needs skills his forerunners would have marveled at.

Al releases the helicopter's stays, and wheels it out. The day is clear and bright. He oils the structure carefully. Now he checks the machinery with a scrupulous eye, then, offering me a hand, helps me into the cabin bubble and buckles me into my seat. His logbook entries tell, like a diary, where he's been, with whom, and why. *Quo vadis?* (Where are you going?) we used to greet one another on campus, the usual answer to which was *Quo vadimus*? (Where are any of us going?). But my favorite answer was *Vide unde venio* (Look where I come from). For Al, the "where I come from" is down in ballpoint.

It would take ages to check each rocky incline and mesa pass on horseback, so Al will scout the tricky sections by air. He shows me how to prop my boots up on the training pedals, and how to hold the training stick (as if I were delicately corraling a butterfly), so I can learn what flight *feels* like. Every tremble of the controls repeats in my hands. The engine revs, and up we whoosh, long-tailed as a dragonfly; we climb, hover, and bank. Below, a herd of antelope explodes into flight, looking jackrabbit-small, their white tails twitching. The land seems good for this time of year—green and grassy. How well the cows will feed. The fences and telephone wires are barely visible. Our shadow could give a dozen cowboys shade.

"Look there," Al shouts over the loud buzz of the engine, and points to a few cowboys working cows. We bank hard, and fly toward them, Al jockeying the foot pedals, stick, and throttle with such ease you'd think he were neck-reining his palomino. Down we plunge to turn the herd, which breaks into a gentle lope. "Running" the herd is a strict no-no, since cattle are sold by the pound. But Al grins despite himself, and half of my flesh feels left behind as we climb suddenly, level out, and head for a nearby mesa to scout strays along the fence line. The fences, which seem to stretch forever across slippery rock plateaux and into floody creekbeds, were put up by a "fence gang" who lived in tents while they spent each day stringing wire, coming into headquarters only once a week or so for supplies. "Gypsies" they were called, and a gypsy life it must have been.

Al banks right to skirt a sandy cliff, the face of which looks blasted smooth by wind and water. I know we're being useful, saving horsemen time, but what a sensual spree the flight is! So close to the air and high are we, I must keep reminding myself that I'm in a craft. I dare not spread my wing-arms like a black-haired eagle, and lean out into the hot prairie air, my hands as finger-fringed as any bird of prey. Al is grinning, and it occurs to me that my mouth is hanging open, as indeed it has been since we took off. An electrocardiogram I would surely fail, so fluttery is the pace of my heart. Below me the ranch, *his* ranch, is a quilt of grazing lands in all directions, a ring of agate mesas, and tiny buildings I have not yet come to recognize. We fly over the remains of an old stone house of the sort I've seen in many isolated places. Always they fill me with such terrible sadness for the people who once lived there, raised families, farmed a few vegetables out back, and left behind only rubble, over which a poet and a rancher might one day inadvertently fly.

To see the mesas strewn with boulders, and spewed-up, shattered, twisted rocks is to know what violence moved here. Imagine water, cool in the early morning, when it dances over a few mossy flat rocks, pours through a loose web of twigs and, splashing gently against one bank, tugs a grain or two of sand into its silky ripple, a grain or two of mud. How it stretches the mind to see massive, gorgeous undulations of rock, and know they were carved by something as lucid as water, something as full of punch and yet invisible as wind. *Imagine it, Diane*, I counsel myself, at once student and teacher, *picture the grain-by-grain chiseling away of those sky-climbing rock strata below you, the ones that are like dark rolls of belly flesh, live the millennia.* I do so, and the next single second blooms into a lifetime of geological thoughts.

An odd pedaling of my feet brings me back to attention. Al has changed direction, and my feet, on the training controls, follow his.

"Want to take over?" he asks.

Too frightened to speak, I nod my head vigorously. I want to fly. The stick, which I've been holding as softly as Rima held birds in *Green Mansions*, I grip firmly, pressing it just a shade to the right. But I am so cautious, the helicopter barely moves. Al urges me to be bolder; I pull back on the stick and climb, climb, drift to the left, feel as if my air-skirts are swaying beneath me, dive a little, slowly and with care, since we are too close to the ground for emergency maneuvers. I want to cry out, but am dumbstruck with cold thrill. I am a condor. I am a kite. I am a weather balloon rising on a gust of air. Giving the controls back to Al, I sit and shake for a few minutes. I am in love with flying. Later I ask for another turn at the controls, this time for a little longer, and feel as if I am skiing on the cool, blue sky-waters. No wonder Antoine de Saint-Exupéry was smitten enough to fly mailplanes across the woolliest Moroccan deserts. No wonder men gave up their ghosts barnstorming over the wheat-gold Nebraskan fields.

"Keep an eye out for eagles," Al warns, "they'll attack."

"Attack?" I ask incredulously. "Attack *us*? What bravado!"

"They're the largest bird, and haven't got any natural enemies, so they just don't know any better."

"If I were the size of an eagle, and something the size of a helicopter came at me, *I* would know better," I insist. "Of course, birds aren't known for their scintillating intellects."

Because I've little idea what works what, I fiddle with the controls. Flash Gordon had a less complex panel.

"Go over that way," Al suggests, and schools me in the maneuver. I edge the stick to the right, press a pedal, and over we go, except that we keep climbing. The tendency *is* to climb, to grab the stick in a death-hold and pull it to your bosom, so I judge the craft's angle off the horizon, as I'm taught to, and bring it back down to a cozy height.

Al, who lets me try everything, is as generous with his trust as he is with his knowledge. And perhaps that best characterizes him: he has faith in people. For him, a human being is a creature that under stress can rise to all occasions, at the best of times excel, and at the worst of times perform nobly. Al respects other men, and he respects himself. Consider how much longer it takes to get a job done, when first he must teach me to do poorly what he and his men have done expertly for years. I am a clumsy *vaquera*. But he teaches me as he would any new hand. It is his job to instruct his men; his duty is to teach them the skills they will live by. And Al has a reputation for doing things the right way, carefully, thoroughly, without cutting corners. There is no substitute for quality workmanship. Just as, for Sherrie, there is no substitute for quality living. Everything around the ranch is scrupulously clean. Metal bootscrapes are recessed into the cement outside the cookhouse, and nobody enters a room with chaps on.

Every floor, sink, wall, table, and surface is scrubbed shiny, clean, and often. No one goes to dinner without a shower and clean clothes. Lynda dons school clothes and curls her hair with a curling iron before trotting across the road to the schoolhouse each morning. And every night, after a day of horn-branding in a mud-sludgy corral, splattery red paint, and sprays of cow feces over clothes, face, and boots, the Mitchell boys come to dinner looking tidy and well dressed as any college students sitting down to a fraternity meal. Their manners are complex, casual, and a delight. I never sit down to dinner that Tom (usually on my right) doesn't hold my chair for me, and push it in with a well-practiced touch. If a woman leaves the table, all the men rise. No fuss. The Mitchell children take etiquette for granted. A woman is to be treated like a lady, even if she insists on riding with the cowboys, and that means letting her step through a doorway before you, saying "excuse me" if you happen to cross the room in front of her, being attentive, protective, and chivalrous. Without trying, they give me the Southern Belle treatment, and I love it.

The good life for the Mitchells also means shopping in the big city, plenty of art and music, ultramodern appliances, and frequent family trips (sometimes in a camper van) to such places as Disneyland or the Jet Propulsion Laboratory. They could be a family living in the middle of Cincinnati.

We set down in a pasture where Tom and Mike are working cows. The grass blows away from us in all directions, and the cows now amble with a purpose. Surely Tom is riding my own horse, Prince, whom I've finally come to recognize: a deep chestnut with a clean white diamond on his forehead, a down-pointing **K** on his left shoulder and, at the moment, a small healing cut on his left flank. Both cowboys move stock gingerly down the fence. Another mile or so, and they'll blend herds with Tony and Navor, then, *en masse*, press on to the next team, and so on, until all the men meet to move the longest and toughest leg of the drive together.

Al and I scream to one another over the helicopter's thunder. Leaning out of the copter door, he signals his intentions by hand, traffic-cop style. Mike is to continue on and Tom ride back. It *is* Prince, I notice as Tom approaches, and so I leap out of the craft in my purple chaps and red boots, my straw hat with scarves that tie under the chin, my tinted sunglasses, and my camera. Tom swings a leg over the saddle and steps down. It could not be called a "dismount," anything that easy; he does it like stepping backward off a curb. Silently, I take Prince's reins and mount up, letting Tom fly back with his dad. Ducking his head as he darts under the flashing blades, he disappears into the blue bubble.

"Thank you," I scream over the helicopter's roar, exaggerating each word so he'll be able to lip-read me at least. But my eyes are dancing like sun-flecked water; their words are unmistakable. I salute loosely as the craft lifts off, then jog toward the fence to join Mike. I wonder if he is still mad at me, or indeed if Al has arranged this rendezvous to spawn a truce. After all, I made a sizable gaffe yesterday. Pranking on the Tequesquite is a way of life, a diversion with unstated ground rules and banter. It's usual, for instance, to hide someone's boots while he or she's eating. The boots never move far—across the room, on a high shelf, under a newspaper, in a cupboard. And everyone knows where the hiding places are. Yesterday, they very naturally hid my boots on me—three times, to my deepening distress. But, as an outsider, what I didn't understand is that boots are never hidden so that they can't be found. The first time, outraged, I'd tramped out into the mud and rain with my socks on, "like a hornet," as Mettie said, pounded on the bunkhouse door, and screamed, "Mettie, I'm going to kill you! Give me my boots!"

He, of course, didn't have them. According to custom, he'd left them in the cookhouse, for someone else to return quickly as soon as I went outside. Later, in open retaliation, I stole a pair of boots I thought were Mettie's from outside the bunkhouse, tossed them into my pickup truck, *and left*. Only after an hour did I find out they were Mike's boots, that he was looking all over the yard for them, and getting ready to steam like a geyser, which Russell warned me of in parabolic understatement: "Mike is just a touch mad about his boots." Mike was seething, in fact, raging and furious. Mike was like a dam ready to burst. He eyed me with a look that could slice bread, snarled and snapped and spit venom. And no apologizing or explaining would soothe him.

"Shoot, shoot, and double shoot," I cursed, realizing how hopelessly I'd misread the prank. Breaking the rules was breaking the world order. Mike slammed the screen door behind him as he stormed into the bunkhouse.

"Have you forgiven me yet?" I ask tentatively.

Mike looks down at the dark, sweaty neck of his horse, shrugs, and with a smile says, "I already forgot it."

"Anyway," I offer, "you owe me one, okay?"

He grins. "If I owe you one, you better watch out!"

He's right, on his turf I'm an innocent. Mike has evidently slept off the mood that soured him. Into his cap, he has threaded a broad eagle feather of the quill-pen variety, and, sizing up his slender, muscle-quilted frame, you might guess that he'd earned the feather Indian-brave style. Even under a long-sleeved western shirt, the span of his chest seems enormous. His dark hands look strong enough to cowboy all by themselves.

Silence prevails, for no special reason but the distance at which we must naturally work. Another team appears on the horizon, and another soon after, until we become a moaning sea of beef. Smiles and waves. With our herds blended, we are a band of seven: Mike, Lynda, Tony, Juan, Terry, Navor, and I. Tony, like R. J., is an oldtime cowboy who has been working on the ranch for most of his life. When Al was five, Tony was only nineteen, and he just about raised him, as Al likes to explain with affection and gratitude. Now Tony lives in Mosquero, a small village nearby, with his wife who grew up in Mosquero just as he did. A music teacher from "the East," New York City to be exact, has just come to settle in the lilliputian town, much to the delight of its culture-starved citizens. Like English teachers, music marms are not plentiful in such rugged country. Tony's daughter lives in Pittsburgh, and he shines when he tells how she'll be bringing her children West for the rodeo next month. Neither of Tony's sons is a cowboy. A lovely man: amiable, wiry, deeply tanned (with an almost permanent forehead stripe by now from so many years out of doors), he's range-wise and thoroughly bilingual. All of his life he's spent on horseback, acquiring the deep sun lines that give his face the drama of a freshly ploughed field.

"You've been with the ranch so long, Tony," I say as we slowly move the herd, "you must have seen a lot of changes in it."

"Oh, yes," Tony says, tilting his head toward me but not

his eyes, like a motorist being cautious about the road. "These days a rancher really has to know business and economics. Ranching has changed so much."

"And how to fly planes. . . ."

"Yes, and all sorts of new things about doctoring and nutrition and genetics. A lot of changes."

His reins he holds as lightly as a bouquet of flowers.

"You probably think I get lonely working out here, but I don't. There's always lots to do. You're outside, you're usually working with other cowboys. And anyway," his eyebrows gently rising to say *it's quite obvious*, he smiles, "the kind who get lonely don't stay cowboys."

A cow breaks loose a few yards away, and Tony trots briskly to drive it back into the herd. Did he neck-rein his horse? If so, I never saw it, so relaxed were his movements, so whispery the signals to his horse.

It was 7:30 when I joined Mike in the pasture, and now, at 10:30, we still have a gigantic distance to cover. The day is hot and dry. The sun could not be fiercer. As they redden, my bare arms look scoured by wire brushes. Together, we drift the cows along the fence line until we reach a pasture gate. But funneling a big herd through a tiny door isn't easy. We form a roomy circle around the cows, pray they won't spook, churn around, and bolt. The air feels tense as a hair trigger. One at a time, the cows trot warily to the gate, hesitate, and jog through. No one moves suddenly, or speaks loudly. One cow stops short, shies, and hightails it into the brush. Juan darts after it and, swinging wide around, works the cow back into the herd, at the same time trying not to run it too hard. It's great sport riding hell-for-leather after an errant cow, and I get a shade better at it as the day progresses, but it seems I've an endless amount to learn before that shade grows resolute as a skill.

Loosening my throat, I yip and yelp after the cows, warble

and cry, make sounds that Latin-band singers would surely
follow with shouts of *Arriba! Arriba!*, no trace of inhibition
about hollering to the herd. What I can't do is whistle as
nimbly as the cowboys do, though by mid-afternoon I wish
I could. In the mornings, people whoop and holler a great
deal, but when fatigue sets in so do the clucks and whistles.
The cows, too, are draggy and don't need such iron-fisted
handling. They seem droolly and tired; along the roadway
are patches of saliva. We rest them for half an hour at regular
intervals, by making a wide circle and standing still as chess
figurines.

Mike stretches out lengthwise atop his horse, tilts his
feathered hat down over his eyes, and snoozes. Lynda jogs
up and bids me join her for a "coffee break." We try to find
a secluded spot, but there is none. Her eyes are keener, and
soon she notices a shallow depression in the land, toward
which we lope. Lynda rides adroitly, and knows her horses
well, is safe and frolicsome and relaxed in the saddle, but is
still too little to mount by herself. So I leg her up, and back
we breeze. Although I'm used to hitting the grass when nature
calls, it's never with company squatting beside me. I've often
wondered what sort of idle conversation men make standing
at urinals, and now I know.

Mike has dismounted, and, sitting in the shadow of his
horse, he looks cooler. The cows bawl less. The air hangs
straight down. Then Tony gives the sign, and we start up the
herd. Few people holler; the air fills with whistles.

I try whistling the theme song from *The Good, the Bad,
and the Ugly*, that staccato, macho ballad about a soft-spoken
good guy and the desperadoes, thinking perhaps a structure
might give my whistle a little oomph. But it's no use, my
whistling is lousy, and you really can't cowboy without
knowing how to whistle well, since, for the cowboys, whistling
is both a hobby and a crucial skill. They whistle to keep

themselves company as they ride, and they whistle to the herd. They whistle most every day, fluently and with a singer's range.

"What's that sound?" I'd asked Al when, in the helicopter, I'd heard a long steady ringing so eerie I'd thought perhaps it was a vibration in the craft or, in my head, a steel hoop singing on the pavement.

"I'm just whistling," he'd said, surprised that it would surprise me, and, with his lips unpuckered and so thinly parted I would have thought it impossible for him to make any sound at all, he resumed. Everyone whistles differently, but there are three kinds of whistles: the round-mouthed whistle (which I do); the two-fingers-splayed-at-the-mouth whistle (which few do, because they need one hand to hold the reins and the other perhaps to wave at the cows), and the thin-mouthed whistle, which is strong, plaintive, and reminiscent of a desert bird. Don sometimes carries a bird whistle with him, just for fun, with which he chirps and sings to the cattle; but its tune is almost too natural to stir them. Tony barks at the cows in a raspy-throated way that sounds *exactly* like an angry pheasant. (I know because in Ithaca a pheasant stalks our woods, driving off neighbor dogs with its vocal displays.)

Overhead, the helicopter occasionally buzzes: Al checking the mesas while his men work the flatlands. Funneling the herd through another pasture gate, we this time emerge beside a highway. And what a bugbear it is to get cows to cross pavement! Everything frightens them: the clatter of their hooves, the incline, the oncoming trucks that wait patiently for our migration to pass. On either side, a deep culvert makes the chore even tougher. All we seem to do for half an hour is chase bawling, obtuse calves out of ditches, and nag, nag, nag the cows across the road, into the culvert on the other side. Idly, I begin to mimic the cow's moo (rather well, I might add, since cow-parody is nothing to flaunt), which sends

Mike and Terry into ripples of laughter, and spawns an afternoon's worth of ribbing about what breed of heifer I might be. They conclude that since, clearly, I'm not a registered cow, Mike and Mettie should flank and brand me.

"Gittalong, Diane," Terry laughs as he herds a many-nippled, hide-swinging Hereford.

I swat him as I would a pesky fly, a teasing brother.

Mike calls casually to the cows, but just as his call ends, I mimic it, adding a perverse drawl. He and Terry don't wait a second. They are after me at a gallop, spreading a rope between them as they ride, drifting six or seven feet apart, and threatening to do something hellish to spooky Prince. Volcanos don't erupt faster than I do into a panicky gallop; I've no idea what's in store, but I know it can't be good with such grins warping their faces. Off we race, until Tony yells at us to stop messing around and get back to work. Grabbing my saddle horn with one hand, I pull Prince back with the other. Giggles from the rear. God knows I'm no expert at riding fast in a western saddle, and even so measured a stop sends me bouncing, stirrups awry. Back to work I get, between Terry and Mike, who grabs my chaps leg and tries to toss me over the saddle, legs angled like a compass. To get even, I catch at his back girth, hoping to surprise him with an impromptu bronco ride. Terry, whom I'd give the world to see at twenty-five, so absolute is his energy and mischief, urges me to rest my feet high over the saddle horn, then dig my heels into the horse's shoulders.

"Horses really like that," he says, a grin creeping up his face like sunlight on a mesa. He tries hard to look angelic.

I'm in for trouble, I know, but my curiosity always leads with its chin. Keeping the reins in one hand and the saddle horn in the other, I tap both heels gently on Prince's shoulders. His back arches like a piece of wood being broken, and he throws in a few small bucks for good measure. Laughs echo around. Terry razzes me again about being built like a heifer, and, though it shouldn't, the teasing stings me. Ranch humor, when it isn't slapstick, is often deriding. A gentle ribbing is not a lampoon, not the fabled stuff grudges are built on, just a bit of innocent shadow-boxing, cowpokes "poking fun" instead of cows. Though on the surface the humor seems spontaneous, its social role is clear. So large and close-living is the ranch family, safety valves abound. But this one, good-naturedly jousting, works especially well at airing real (or imagined) shortcomings, unfamiliar or downright strange habits. Revealed, one is liberated, made to feel acceptable despite one's eccentricities. Ribbing, flirtation, and sibling-tease overlap, though rarely do the ranch boys and girls date one another.

On the other hand, as in most cultures, some topics are so sensitive and tense only humor can touch them: death, class distinctions, racial prejudice, sexual problems. I'm not surprised to learn that Spanish euphemisms for death are just as colorful as their English counterparts. When you die, you can "stretch your legs" (*estirar las patas*), "hang up your tennis shoes" (*colgar los zapatos de tenis*), "twist your tail" (*retorcer la cola*), simply "disappear" (*desaparecer*), or, as if you were just out strolling, "turn the corner" (*doblar la esquina*), and vanish into life's final shop.

Though the Tequesquite's humor has a basic slant, the style of each of its practitioners varies. Al's humor is usually tinged with irony, Sherrie's with understatement, Lynda's with a giggly love for the absurd, Terry's prankish, Rachel's lasciv-ious, and so on. In my world, humor is pun-laden wit: swift, allusive, and, usually, barbless; or, when aimed at a foe, rapier-smooth—but in both cases clearly academic. We are word-people with bulging vocabularies, not people of action, and we live, love, joke, duel, and woo with words. Far tougher than learning how to work on a cattle ranch is learning how to be funny in their terms. Indeed, how even to be interesting.

8

Cows drift behind sunflower curtains as they graze. Lynda and Rachel are still singing "Sunflower, Good Morning." Some of the cowboys practice roping by trying to lasso a sunflower's bright, haloed head. Everyone is sunflower-struck. Even those who claim to be indifferent I catch going out of their way to ride through a pool of the tall flowers, or idly pluck at petals while they rest the herd. In northeastern New Mexico, it's unusual to find any flowers at eye level. The breeze that picks up around mid-afternoon makes the sunflowers ripple like yellow velvet being stroked. When the breeze stiffens, they shake and roll on their flimsy stems. Already the cows know to hide behind the flowers when it's round-up time. And how startled they seem when, unannounced, a cowboy leaps through the yellow curtain! An illusion Cocteau would have loved.

My thighs ache so badly that I cannot walk upright. Now I understand why cowboys are always depicted as being bow-legged. It's not sitting with your legs bent around a horse all day that does it, but the stirrup's tendency to break the ankle out, which stretches the entire leg muscle up to the thigh.

My mental muscles ache, too; books, paintings, music, science, philosophy—nothing I've spent so long learning pertains to the muscle-and-sweat obbligato of each day, the physical reasoning with an errant cow or spooky herd, the complex analysis of a windmill carried out by a keen eye taught, from childhood, how to read the land like a text and machinery like an organism that can be cured. I am not out of my depth but in a different ocean, where all things look familiar, but are different, and even basic physics seems odd enough to make you reach for the chair arm when you sit down.

Then why on earth should I come here and, having come, why care so soul-splittingly about these strangers who could no more understand me than I them, who baffle easily when I speak in my normal way, so that I'm forever pruning and bankrupting my thoughts, and to whom I surely seem humorless, brash, unfeminine, unqualified. Why need to do the dirtiest, sweatiest work? Why not be content to stay home in Ithaca, where I can rise late and trot down to the study with a mug of coffee to stoke my brain-fires for the day, where friends can be counted on to get even the worst of my puns, and acceptance, when it comes, comes in the mail? What am I doing in this far-flung world, why does it exalt and chasten me in turns, and how have I moved so quickly from plain curiosity to this desperate need to belong? Why do Sherrie and Al—he, younger than my husband; she, the same age as many of my girlfriends—seem so much older, so parental? Surely it isn't they who orchestrate these roles, but *my* need for their parenting. So many questions. Alice in her Wonderland was less puzzled by the forces that drove her.

As the orange half-light of sunrise trots through the corrals like a nervous colt, I head for the cookhouse as usual, but this time find Mettie jacking up my pickup truck out back instead of wrangling the day's horses. Barely awake, I run over to see what trouble I've gotten into now, and discover a tire so flat it looks like it was designed that way to stay put: a rubber sculpture. According to the ranch's cardinal rule, whatever goes wrong in your keeping you fix. It makes for more responsible handling, I'm sure, and includes everything from your truck to the windmills in the pastures you patrol. Only, thanks to some benign dispensation of the fates, I've never had to fix a flat tire before; to me, *jack* is just a name. Still, I must offer.

"Aiii, Mettie, I've got a flat, huh?"

Looking up, he shakes his head in that gesture of combined amusement, put-outedness, and disbelief I seem to cause frequently in the course of my stay. In his eyes, I read, *The day hasn't even begun yet! And already you're a handful.*

"It's my truck," I sigh, "I'm the one who should fix it. Is there a manual in the glove compartment?" Visions of a morning spent decoding the instructions. I curse myself soundly in the rising light. Mistress of ranch skills I don't expect to be, but how I wish I knew enough at least not to make extra work for the cowboys.

"It's okay," Mettie says, "I'm just jacking it up, not fixing it. Someone else will do that. Anyway, it's only flat on one side." He goes after his own truck.

Minutes later, the "only flat on one side" line registers, and clears some of my guilt with a laugh.

Since Mettie must go to Tucumcari for truck repairs, and Sherrie needs to fetch supplies, they decide to travel in tandem so Mettie can do the heavy lifting and carrying. A new clothes dryer heads Sherrie's list, followed by dry goods, food, medicine, and beauty items. Notebook in hand, she makes her rounds like a colonial merchant, taking orders for store-bought things. Whispers from most buildings make it clear the one thing nearly everybody needs is Kotex.

"Sure you don't need anything?" she asks, as solicitous as

one must be when *town* is a faraway abstraction.

"No, no," I assure her, "I'm a walking pharmaceutical company." And I am: creme rinse, Sominex, Midol, poison-ivy gel, purges and solidifiers, decongestants and astringents . . . no one could survive all the emergencies my kit has cures for.

Sherrie adds two last-minute requests to her list: Mike's for some paraffin to treat his rope with, and (very much to my surprise) Don's for a book called *Psychocybernetics*. She jumps into her gold-dust-colored Ford T-bird; Mettie climbs into his black truck with the muraled windows. And together they leave like a caravan pulling out, in a long dusty squall, to bring back the riches of civilization. Not exactly frankin-cense and myrrh, perhaps, but every bit as luxurious and awaited.

Lynda and I, in Rachel's mini-pickup, decide to help the cowboys spread vitamins and salt nearby. Slowly, over pock-marked terrain, we drive to the wooden feed-hods, and there shoot the breeze till cowboys come to pour minerals and drag sacks to more distant depots. Lynda's skin, though it's tinged red-brown from the sun, has all the silkiness of a ten-year-old complexion, is clear as creek water, smooth as a new bolt of cream-colored cloth. She is all little girl, all on the surface; and I smile to see her sitting so self-composed and casual, inured to the deep, rich odor of the stinkweed I find as strong as civet glands, as she tells me of her daily doings. This is the same girl I've seen color like a thermometer when she over-heats.

"And *eeee*," she says excitedly about pulling calves, "it's like you're helping to bring them into the world." Her knowl-edge of midwifery sobers me; children around livestock learn the quite complex facts of life wonderfully early. Myself, as I recall, I kept my illusions until I was seventeen when, dip-ping into a psychology textbook, I was astounded to learn how reproduction works. And my mother, growing up in a large immigrant family on the Maryland coast, at a time when sexual ignorance was good breeding, thought for many years that babies were vomited. She'd once half-seen a cat giving birth, noticing that, each time the mother cat retched, a baby kitten appeared; no one disabused her. And what her mother did for information, heaven knows. Although perhaps it's only city-dwelling in-betweeners like us, my mother and me, who live too far from animals to know how animals work. Grandma had some small livestock in Austria (chickens and goats, perhaps) and Great-grandma a slightly fuller farm where she sold sugar to men playing dominoes, and embroidered vests, both to raise money for what was then the ultimate extravagance: educating her children.

Rachel splits the silence with her CB version of a hotfoot: turning her radio up full-blast and holding the mike against it so the blaring rock hits hard over nearby truck speakers. Lynda and I cringe. Our eyelids roll up. Then Lynda giggles and asks Rachel what's doing.

Apparently, a buyer is due on the ranch any time now, someone interested in one of the prime bulls grazing in the pasture across the road. Cowboys have already begun trotting in from other fields. A roil of dust down the road means Al's pickup, though it probably won't arrive for ten or fifteen minutes. Into a pasture full of leviathan bulls we bump, shock absorbers doing the best they can. At a safe distance from the herd, I press a button on the dashboard that works a loud, screechy siren: Pavlovian, not apocalyptic. The bulls come to the truck's siren to be fed. Over each one, a black mass of flies floats like a thundercloud.

9

Late one night, as I'm seated in the Mitchells' den with Sherrie, Al, and all the children, swapping a few insights about our diverse lives, Mike raps gently on the door. Dressed in a clingy white shirt and fresh trousers, he walks tentatively through the kitchen, his hair newly combed and his dusty face washed. Tonight he looks even taller than his six feet five inches, and decades older than twenty-one. Al and Sherrie exchange inquiring glances, then the three of them disappear into Al's office, from which, only a moment later, comes Sherrie's short, pained sigh. Outside, we're like a courtroom guessing what's transpired in the judge's chambers. Our mood grows even heavier as drinks are delivered to the office in a steady stream, and it's clear the conversation, whose dark mumbling we hear, will continue for a long while.

"Growing pains," Sherrie says affectionately when Mike's left. "He wants to go with the W— Ranch, the one owned by Tenneco. And that's such a horrible place for him to be, I told him I wouldn't give him a good reference if they called.

I'd tell them he was a pretty sorry cowboy," she says, drawling the last four words until they sound like an abomination on the prowl. *A pretty sorry cowboy.*

"That's no place for Mike! A dude ranch where executives pay fortunes to have cowboys guide them while they shoot homegrown stock, then have the cowboys spit and shine their boots each night. They'd chew Mike up and ruin him. I'd sooner lose him to anyplace but there," she says, and looks flushed with worry as she plops down in her usual armchair. With a smile, Al collects Lynda, who is already snoozing, and carries her off to bed, but strain is tight as a cinch across his face.

That Mike should want to see the world a bit is no surprise to anyone. Actually, he hasn't been on the ranch very long: only since May. But he's settled in fast, works so well; it's hard to think of the ranch without Mike on it, an eagle feather through his cap. What brought him to the Tequesquite originally was cowboying. For some time he'd worked on a ranch elsewhere that, ultimately, converted its efforts to farming.

"I'll sit in the saddle," Mike said to me over breakfast one day, "but I'm no farmer. I couldn't plough and seed the same land over and over. I'm a cowboy, not a farmer, and a cowboy is a different breed."

Again I hear that tagline—"a cowboy is a different breed" —this time from one of them, and for a moment can't tell if it's self-romanticism or self-awareness that sponsors the phrase. At twenty-one, bright, sensitive, and intense, Mike may well feel cut off from civilization's real and fabled adventures. A familiar itch. And the odds are low that the local, small-town girls will include one with "a little upstairs," as he prefers. He loves skiing, but the ranch is really too far from a snowy oasis to make such jaunts feasible. He might go to college. He might, in fact, move to Santa Fe where he has some women friends. The world is his oyster, but at the moment it's one awash with gritty choices. Curiosity versus security. Drifting versus the ranch's more normal family life. Steady cowboy wages (about $350 a month plus room and board) versus higher but less dependable money. Room and board you can't lose in a poker game, or mortgage. The unexplored, the inviting, the unknowable. Mike wrestles with his angel for some time, then decides to go to the dude ranch after all, the one where cowboys do everything but hold down the antelope for the guests to shoot.

10

Lunch: roast beef, beans, salad, rolls, peas, a bright-yellow "sunflower" iced cake for dessert. Afterward, Tom and Terry drive an elephantine truck around, spraying afflicted trees with insecticide. Though they seem blasé about the vapors, I move upwind, and watch them fog an all-too-sparse stand of trees. Early homesteaders often made "tree claims" on the prairie, but few guessed how quickly the climate would undo their labors. On some trees, there's even a high Plimsoll line, thanks to the desperate grazing of livestock. One rarely thinks of trees on the New Mexico flats but, especially as you move up the mesas, there are many: pinyon, ponderosa pine, one-seed juniper, wavy-leaf oak, cottonwood, willow, and others, few of them hearty, most of them plagued by the drought or never-ending chain of insects. Just listen to the winged canticles of early morning, sounding now like a baroque choir and now like an angry mob, and the sheer *throng* of insect life, at once so multiple and shrill, will astound you. Crickets of all sorts, katydids, tumblebugs (dung beetles that, unwit-

115

tingly, fertilize the soil by burying dung balls), grasshoppers that can grow to lengths of three inches and ravage acres; blowflies, carrion beetles and other adroit converters of dead flesh to energy; butterflies, bees, moths, leafhoppers, walking-sticks, and other pollinators, uncountable aphids, honeybees (like the horse and the cow: at first imported from the Old World), native bees that neither socialize nor store honey but do sting, vociferous and benign ants too diverse and numerous to give more than a cold shiver to. Also parasites and worms, maggots and mosquitos, gnats, spiders, true flies, and things with carapaces I no longer know even how to classify.

While Tom and Terry continue their blitz on the leaf-suckers, Mettie and Juan load salt into the back of a truck, then, their radio lyricizing the complaint of a troubled house-wife, they bounce across the cattle guard and off to the pastures. Mike, who with Don rounded up stock all morning, giving them bags of feed cake to supplement the prairie grasses, now rests in the bunkhouse with his troubles.

Though siesta time is over, I've not yet been called to duty, so I climb onto the top rail of the corrals, my favorite perch, and sun myself while I jot notes. It's not the height exactly I find so appealing, though the top slat of the corral is just high enough both to scout the creekbed and keep out of reach of the ground-preferring flies. I like watching the distant hills, the sandy creek walls, and the grasslands beyond, the barbed-wire fence trailing into the distance like a rust-red cord. Most of all, I love watching the horses in the corral: mixing, drinking, rippling their flanks, swishing their tails like punkah wallahs, sniffing at the dust, cribbing gently on bits of wood, resting as I do between jobs.

Far across the corrals, I see Mike tossing his saddle into his pickup truck, and I jump down with a cry, wanting to catch him before he leaves.

"You're going then?" I ask sadly.

He squints in the glare. "No, just for the weekend."

"You're not going then. You seemed so sure an hour ago."
I try to sound neutral, but am far from it. I like this shy, sensitive cowboy, and shudder to think of the dude-ranch deg-
radation Sherrie had described. There is such a delicate spirit
in Mike; I hear sometimes he just gets into his car and drives
for long hours, headed nowhere.

"I was telling Don all morning I was going," he laughs,
"but I figure I can wait till the snow falls." He tosses the rest
of his gear into the truck, and seems sad, as if he knows
nothing has really been settled, or could be.

"Your gear?"

"I'm just going to my grandfather's for the weekend." He
shows me a copper-bitted bridle he's just made. It looks lovely
—handcrafted and new.

The Mitchells have offered to send Mike to college, if he
likes, one nearby where he could learn something about
ranching, with a view perhaps to one day being a foreman
somewhere. If Russell is any indication, foremen have a lot
more paperwork to do than people guess, and spend as much
time riding the desk as the range. Still, foreman or manager
is really the highest a cowboy can aspire to, since owning a
ranch takes the sort of money one usually marries into or
inherits.

I bid Mike a good weekend and watch him drive away,
then I start climbing back up on the corral fence, to scout the
ever-changing and changeless prairie, when Mettie and Juan
suddenly return, wolf-whistling to get my attention. Mid-
climb, I spin round to greet them.

"Going to Logan for the weekend?" I ask brightly.

Mettie shrugs his shoulders at the easy mischief. "Maybe.
Depends on the weather."

From the cookhouse's screened porch, Susie sights us, and
points to me sitting cross-legged on the corral, saying loudly

to someone hidden in the shadows what sounds like "Wunner-woo."

Juan starts to giggle, and pulls his cap down over his face.

"What's she calling me?" I ask Mettie. But he swears he doesn't know.

11

An afternoon visit with Al's Aunt Betty (his dad's sister) —a spunky, self-reliant, scrappy, frontier woman whose speech includes hard-as-nails cussing as well as finely polished expressions in French—is an object lesson in hardiness. In her stone house, furnished with heavy old Spanish chests, frame beds, antiques, animal skins, and simple tables, the low ceilings and cell-like rooms contribute to the sense one gets of being in a turn-of-the-century monastery near the Mexican border. She prefers to live without a telephone or TV, has minimum help to run the place, and seems perfectly at home in the open, old-fashioned kitchen where an enormous bunch of threaded peppers hangs like a museum exhibit. "They're just drying," she says, as I gape at the fire-red shield of peppers cringing and growing even brighter as they dry. "Are they real?" I hear myself asking, and, lifting a hand to feel at their waxy topography, let it pause in mid-air. Of course they're real. Not one of Georgia O'Keeffe's lush desert flowers. Nor am I the first to be smitten by their pageantry. In December, Betty will braid them into flaming Christmas wreaths. But now they look like a food sculpture in a *cordon bleu* kitchen, or something from the center of a star.

Dinner at the Mitchells' (lasagna, Spanish style) begins with cocktails and ends with a mixed-media dessert Lynda and Rachel have confected from a stumbled-upon recipe. Looking at its shapes and shimmers in the pan, I'm reminded of Betty's larder full of home preserves—everything from bread and butter pickles to cactus jelly. Kept in a cool, damp room, the jars had looked thick with alchemical tonics: chunks of green floating in a speckly gel, brown liquid tinged with iridescence, clear orange oil, mummified fruits, ropy brews.

It's Lynda's turn to say grace, and she begins by thanking God for my safe arrival, which moves me deeply with its simplicity and concern. We are all thankful, on the cows' behalf, for the rain, and urgently plead the *Logos* for even more. Then, as head of the household (and table), Al serves. Plates of bread and butter, salad and dressings, change hands. Rachel brings in tall glasses of water and milk. Naturally, our visit to Aunt Betty dominates the talk. She is one tough dame, feisty as hell, whether she's taking on the low-flying Air Force jets or judging cattle at a large, rough-and-tumble stock show. Rumor has it that one day, when she was younger, she did a Godiva number on the horizon during round-up, just to keep the cowhands on their toes. I suggest a troika for her winter travels, and can see her bundled up in black animal-skins, a flask or two on board, as she sails at whip-cracking speed across the snowy dunes.

Rain again after dinner. Lynda and Rachel wade out to the schoolhouse in the dark, and back through mud and swampy brush with me, so I can make a phone call from the cook-house. With Lynda in the middle, clutching both of our arms, we slip and slide, giggle, and sing every song we can remember the words to, "Margaritaville" and "The Battle Hymn of the Republic" among others, hopelessly straining for a compatible pitch. A firefly dogs my steps and I finally stop swatting at it when I realize it's the moon reflecting in each puddle as we pass. At the bunkhouse, common sense rules, and we muffle our giggles, whisper our Best of the Hit-Parade, and even tiptoe past the darkened building. Though it's only 9:30, all the cowboys' lights are out. Only the painters, temporarily bunking on the ranch, have the bad sense to be as awake as we are.

12

Juan is a fine vaquero, if a less flashy one than Mettie who seems to act before others even know an action is called for. Juan's cattle yells are mild tempered; Mettie's loud and threatening. After lunch, and siesta-hour spent practicing with a rope, I join Juan, Mettie, Don, and the others at the corral. Their horses they rope and saddle in a trice, while I hold a coiled rope in one hand, crank around the other wrist holding the lasso, and let fly like a lifeguard tossing a preserver into a community pool. Finally, I manage to lasso one of Prince's ears, and that's all it takes to make him give up the battle. "I did it," I say in pure astonishment, before the silliness of the picture settles in: a purple-chapped cowgirl attached by umbilical to her horse's left ear. Giggles from nearby.

"You think it's easy to lasso just an ear!" I yell. "Any fool can lasso a whole neck!"

My bare midriff is wet with the heat. Carrying the saddle and blanket only a few feet steams my arms, which grip each other under the saddle as if it were a leather muff, their bicepses straining to hoist such a weight. As I bend over to catch the dangling girth, my rump high and broad, Mettie rolls a blunt cigar across his teeth, peeks through the slats, and says, *"¡Muy grande!"* then disappears with Terry and Navor, all three hidden by the fence, dust, and shimmer.

Don, silent through the ribbing, as ever, rides with me down to the creekbed, then across a rolling pasture to pick up cows for horn-branding later in the week. On a long, loose rein, we lope for some time across the pasture, letting our horses pick their own way among the yucca and cactus. And I remember hearing about the far-and-wide travels of evangelist John Wesley, who covered 300,000 miles on horseback during his ministry, by buying scruffy horses known to be "stumblers," and riding them on a perilously loose rein, so they could find their own footing (cure themselves, in fact) while he relaxed and piously read the Bible.

Prince occasionally leaps over a prickly yucca, instead of breaking his stride to swerve around it. Finally, we sink to a light trot. Prince gets little work, and is just starting to lather; suds creep through the chestnut fur as if it were a flannel nightdress being delicately washed. So I walk him a bit, while Don jogs ahead. Straight above, the sun shines brutally. Already my never-tanning arms are cherry-red, and the day's work is just starting. So, pulling a long-sleeve blouse from the double set of rawhide taws at the back of the saddle, I tell Don to ride on a few paces while I change, adding, unnecessarily, "And *don't* peek!"

"No, M'am," Don says, his voice a little trembly, "I'm the one person you don't have to worry about peeking." He conscientiously rides on, while I sheathe my sore arms in a tie-dyed yellow blouse, feeling a little gaudy but sunsafe.

At the windmill, where the herd has gathered, Juan appears out of nowhere to help us move the cows, this time riding a creamy palomino.

"Pretty shape," he says with a grin.

"What?" I ask. "Or whose?"

He points to me, still grinning.

"You saw me?" I can't believe it! Nothing, no one was visible anywhere.

Juan laughs, and chases along an inert cow. He must have been on the horizon somewhere, and seen only my unmistakable hat on horseback, the movements of changing a shirt.

"One hundred and eighty thousand acres of prairie," I lament loudly, "and I'd have more privacy in a changing room at Gimbel's."

Don's horse, Glassy, a gray with an eerie, pale eye, throws a fit for no particular reason—the sun maybe, or a shadow—bucking, spinning, and kicking every few minutes. Even so, we get the herd to the waterhole at headquarters, where it'll stay for the night. Juan points to a stranded pickup truck down the road and laughs. Yes, it's mine. The second in two days.

How furious I'd been this morning when, after breakfast, I'd driven back to the school to fetch my chaps, and bogged down in the thick syrupy mud. I'd spun the wheels over and over in their ruts, then finally turned off the ignition and walked down to the corral. Al was just coming around the corner.

"I don't know how to tell you this, Al," I said sheepishly.

"I bet I can guess," he said with a smile.

"I'm sorry."

"That's all right; it happens," he said.

"Yes, but it seems to happen mostly to me. It's my fault, my lack of experience mud-driving; *I'm* the one who'll get it out—promise."

He smiled kindly. "Let's wait till the dirt dries first."

So I'd continued down to the corral, to saddle up and start the day, calling over my shoulder, "You know it's going to take you all winter just to recover from my visit," and hearing Al chuckle as he went about his work.

After leaving the herd at headquarters, we unsaddle our horses. But it's only 3:00, so Don and Juan get out the green metal branding shoot, attach it to the pickup, and haul it into a corral, where they set up for tomorrow's horn-branding. Heavy, clumsy, the squeeze-shoot takes a lot of maneuvering and muscle. By 4:00 we are at last finished, and I can go to the cookhouse to get some cold Kool-Aid from the refrigerator, and chat a while with Adelina and Rachel.

"Wunnerwoo!" Susie claps her hands when I show up. Freshly washed, her damp hair clings to her head like a shiny black helmet and, if anything, she looks even cuter: a diminutive 1920's flapper. With a ceremonious wave, she scampers off to an adjacent room to play. Which, Rachel is dying to know, were the curse words Mettie taught me? She and Adelina start to giggle, a mental checklist in their eyes. As I answer, I discover to my surprise that most of the expressions are euphemisms, not direct references to the body. *Chorro*, which on the ranch is a near synonym for *prick*, in the right circumstances may be complimentary; but more often it's curt, harsh, and spat out in argument like its English counterpart, a bit of obscene flak. What's interesting is that, literally, the word simply means "a large stream," and would be perfectly harmless in other Spanish-speaking areas. Here the synecdoche* *prick* is replaced by a synecdoche itself. I remember hearing one of the cowboys tease a bull with the rhyming tribute, *"Chorro toro."* By this time, Adelina, Rachel, and I are starting to get silly and make up some rhymes of our own, when it occurs to me that *chorro* sounds like first-person of a first conjugation (pun intended) verb running something like: *chorro, chorras, chorra, chorramos, chorráis, chorran.* It's too much; we're belly-laughing now to picture the scene

---

* An English locution in which the part stands for the whole, or vice versa.

each verb form describes. After all, the *-ais* ending is perfectly proper when addressing a saint. Russell appears in the doorway, out of nowhere; he must have been working in an office down the hall.

"You heard . . . . ?

Russell grins. "Yep." Nothing fazes him.

Finally, Lynda shows up and pleads to know what we're all laughing so hard about. Adelina wipes a laugh-tear from one eye, and I try to think of things more decorous. How will Rachel handle this, I wonder, so as neither to inform Lynda prematurely, nor on the other hand to make her feel excluded.

"Oh, we were just talking dirty," Rachel laughs, and when Lynda asks what the words were we were saying, Rachel wisely suggests she guess. Lynda thinks for a moment, then repeats a mild oath she's heard around the ranch.

"That's it!" Rachel nods persuasively. Satisfied, Lynda giggles along with us, one of the pack, and inquires no further.

Adelina and Juan seem as married as people can be, despite their ages. How did they meet? I ask her, and she tells me that in Sabinosa, a beautiful peninsula town she grew up in, Juan one day saw her and her sisters drive past in a car. He had been working for her uncle, as serendipity would have it, and so found out immediately that she was "the little one." He had had the *valor*, as Adelina says, to write her a letter, asking if he might meet her. And though she was only thirteen, she had said yes. They corresponded, exchanged pictures. And then it was arranged that he would come to visit, which he did on horseback, traveling quite a distance. But Adelina, never having been out before, was timid and scarce his whole visit, too shy even to be seen; in time, they both became bolder.

"He's a good man," she says matter-of-factly, with the all-things-considered tone of an older woman in an older culture.

On the way back to the schoolhouse, to scrub for dinner, I find my truck still mired in the drying mud, kick at the crusty earth to test it, and rush with hope when a top layer flakes away like the cracked surface of a brownie. I cross my mental fingers, and climb aboard, start the engine, and slowly rock the truck back and forth until finally, and unexpectedly, it pulls free, the tires climbing out of their four ruts like zombies from the grave. Grinning a back-patting grin, I drive carefully to the schoolhouse, park on a dry rise just beyond the jungle gym, and go in for a shower, feeling inordinately pleased by the minor good fortune. Then, closing the Cyclone-fence gate behind me, freshly washed and cologned, I head for the truck again, and walk straight into the path of an up-coiling snake. Tan, with large black diamonds down its back, thick as my arm, it rises and sways like a Hindu rope. No doubt it's flabbergasted I would come so close, and just as startled as I am. But I know better than to stop and reason with it. Flight takes my legs before my thoughts, and, if possible, I'm running backward to the gate, then hightailing it across the muddy pasture, an equally dangerous route in snake country, vaulting the fence, and racing to the cookhouse where, out of puff, I try to telegraph my alarm.

"Snake! Snake!" I point vaguely toward the schoolhouse, while I catch my breath. I assume the cowboys will not let my fear go unteased, but they are stone sober.

"Where?" Terry asks, jumping up from the table.

"Schoolhouse, by the gate."

"What exactly did it look like?"

Look like. It looked like something from a museum, something in a zoo behind plates of glass. "It was tan with big black diamonds all down its back, and about so high." I motion to mid-thigh.

"This is important," Terry says. "Did it make any noise? Did it rattle?"

Did it rattle. "I don't think so. I'm sure I'd notice if it had."

Terry grabs a broom and hops onto his motorbike, sends dust and gravel flying as he zooms off to find the snake.

"A broom?" I ask, when Terry's dust has cleared. "You

chase snakes with brooms?" I slide into a caricature of Annie
Oakley: "I thought y'all clobbered 'em with six-shooters and
laryits."

Why I should feel so confident about Terry's being able to
handle himself, I really don't know. He's a young boy where I
come from, and, were we on a wooded lot in Pennsylvania, or
walking through the Appalachians, *I'd* be the daring one, re-
sponding instinctively to my role as guardian. Yet with what
breezy permissiveness I let Terry tramp out after a venomous
snake. With what ease I become a little girl, terror's victim,
and run to my big brothers for help, my little brothers even.
Strange. And yet I trust Terry's common sense. It isn't just
that ranch folk know how to gauge their local dangers. It isn't
just that they learn the art of snake-handling early on. I've
never seen the Mitchell children be reckless. Prankish, yes,
cranky or troublesome on occasion, but never blind to immi-
nent danger. Terry may not know how to judge the tempers
of two street-corner hoods in Manhattan, or know which hills
on Cornell's campus are so beset by lightning that not wearing
a rubber raincoat and sneakers during a thunderstorm is tantamount to open suicide, or how to drive hills sheety with ice
along the Finger Lakes, but his knowledge of what can go
wrong around the ranch, his naturalist's training, is so strong
and deeply ingrained I would trust it every time in a crisis.
This sense of sobriety when danger threatens, the high-
adrenalin puzzling out of what needs to be done, I've seen so
often on the ranch it's almost an emotional theme. Terry, too,
has acquired the knack. Even in Lynda there is a caution beyond her years—a governor on the skylarking machine of her
youth, that keeps *safety* always in mind. The rattlesnakes. The
leeches. The wanton horns of squabbling bulls. The insects.
The quicksand. The painful flick of a horse's heel when it's
being saddled. The gopher holes. The slippery inclines, and
the brambles. The chance of sunstroke. The machinery mishaps. Danger is no more a leitmotif on a ranch than it is in a

big city; it's just that nature is ruder and more predictable than people are. A blank face in the Bronx may hide a friend or a thug, but a rattlesnake is always the enemy.

Soon Terry returns with an ear-to-ear grin. It was a bull snake, first cousin and look-alike to a rattlesnake, but non-poisonous. Still, it can bite painfully, often leaving a pair of teeth in the flesh that, in time, will "walk out," as the locals say. Though we never called it "walking out" (I don't think we called it anything, actually), the same thing happened to me my first summer after high school, when I was doing slum clearance work in New York City, and happened to embed a shard of glass in my foot. Years later, it finally "walked out," and, to this day, I'm not exactly sure how such a thing happens, but I suspect it has to do with water pressure in the cells gently pushing a foreign object—a piece of glass, or snake teeth—toward the lighter pressure of the skin surface.

Terry didn't kill the bull snake, which is a fine mouser, just lifted it over the broom handle and moved it down the road a piece to stake out a new territory. Still, I'm cautious when I return to the schoolhouse after dinner, and try to sharpen my hearing to a point fine enough to pick out rattles from the twilight clamor of insects, my sight keen enough to spot diamonds in the tan-and-black-toned shadows. Snake eyes; may I never roll them again.

13

"El sol," Mettie says swinging a casual hand, as we turn a large herd toward the rising sun, and begin the half-day's drive up the mesas to where lush meadows of grass wait behind rock façades. All but Al, who has business at headquarters, are in the saddle; and, as the herd stretches to three or four abreast, cowboys take their positions on either side, the best herdsmen at the head of the column to direct it, and the green-horns like me at the rear to chase along stragglers. I change position often during the morning, riding now mid-herd as we pass tensely through curtains of sunflowers, and now at the head as we scramble over brush and scree. Only much later, and couched in a conversation about something else entirely, will Russell explain what's not apparent to me now: that there is an etiquette to herding cattle. You never get in front of someone else's position, but stay where you're supposed to *vis à vis* the herd and let the next guy look out for himself. To jockey around (besides being like musical chairs) faintly suggests the next person can't patrol his own section. Ignorant

of my bad manners, I scamper from one position to the next, watching how the cows keep track of their young, how the tails swish and thwack against the hide on each flank like the knotted rawhide taws of a penitent, how the cowboys practice roping by trying to lasso jackrabbits on the hop. Nobody has to sing to the herd anymore, as the night-riders did to the dozing, easily spooked cows on the trail where any random noise or sight—a clap of thunder, a cowboy riding out of the shadows on a shimmery evening—might scare the nervous herd into a harrowing stampede. To prevent such a catastrophe, cowboys sang softly to the cows, usually about the things that preoccupied them—keeping the herd quiet, getting the cows to market, as in this verse from one of the songs:

> Oh, say little dogies, when will you lie down
> And give up this shifting and roving around?
> My horse is leg weary, and I'm awfully tired
> But if you get away I'm sure to get fired.
> Lie down, little dogies, lie down
> Hi-yo, hi-yo, hi-yo.

Most of the songs were quiet, slow paced, and a little anxious, a mournful "There, there," the cowboy's bedside manner. And though I'm sure some men made impromptu instruments, the legend of the singing cowboy with a guitar slung over his back and a harmonica in his saddlebags flatly ignores the realities of the life. What a bulky nuisance a guitar would have been on the trail; and a harmonica would have terrorized the cows which, some accounts say, were capable of stampeding at the sound of a match striking. But singing cowboys there were, and it was crucial to their trade. These days I hear no one singing much of anything, and regret the passing of the night-rider's art.

Atop the mesa, the air feels cooler and almost sweet compared to the dusty air below. The grass stands tall enough to hide in, and giant grasshoppers (which Mettie quips are "registered" grasshoppers) make the long stems of the blue grama twitch. Streams run through tight, prickly thickets, and the cows dive almost irretrievably into pockets of young trees. But the best grass lies farther on up the mesa, so after the cows and into the thickets we ride, hats tilted down to keep branches out of eyes, and chaps doing what they were designed for: protecting our legs from the thorns and sharp twigs. A cow standing in the eye of a brambly tornado just peers. I can't get in and she'll be damned if she'll get out. My shouts and sudden lunges don't move her. Don jumps in with all the guts of an aerialist, cracking small branches under him as he ploughs through the thicket, getting close enough finally to chase the cow out. But other cows are disappearing in thickets elsewhere, and the optical illusion of cows and cowboys popping in and out of the landscape is so storybook I shake my head to clear it of what must be an hallucination. A reddish glint behind a scrub oak across the creek is a wayward cow, and Russell lopes down the muddy bank, half of which is overhung by creepers and fallen trees, working his way to the cow like a surfer riding through the tunnel of a wave. Then in a flash the reddish glint becomes half a ton of Hereford scrambling toward the open.

Now and again we pass runs of fence that must be restrung over rocks and across creekbeds. One try at winding barbed wire without gloves teaches me the full meaning of "equipment." Instead I watch as Navor passes a length of stray wire around a rock to secure it, checking the drape and coverage of the fence, as he repairs the work of a flash flood or prowling cow. Where the fence stretches across the creekbed is called a "watergap," and to hear the cowboys talk of it you'd think they were inmates in an asylum bemoaning shock treatment. No job is grumbled about more; I suppose it's the infrequency of the chore as much as anything that gives it such mythic shades of unappeal. Then, too, when the creeks are in flood, and quicksand abounds, it's easy to fall—hat, boots, chaps, and all—into the water. Some of the cowboys don't swim. To Navor, almost every fence on the ranch is familiar, since he started as a "gypsy," one of the fence gang, and has worked for the Mitchells for many years, teaching himself everything he knows about cowboying or, for that matter, reading and writing. Like most cowboys, he's self-educated: a naturalist, a mechanic, an equestrian, an engineer, a stockman. His accomplishments are always visible. That line of fence strung in the brutal white heat of August. The cow he dragged out of a bog beyond the rise. The windmill he ripped out by the roots, as if it were a long gray tooth, and replanted down the road. He lives and works in a sea of his trophies, and each accomplishment, commemorated by a well site or a difficult, shaly climb of fence, stocks his confidence and self-esteem.

Back in the saddle, Russell takes a plug of tobacco from a pouch, and offers it around, including me.

"Okay, I'm game," I say, pinching a bit of damp tobacco between my thumb and first two fingers. "What can it do to me? I used to smoke quite a lot."

The men fold tobacco wads into their cheeks and, as nonchalantly as possible, I do the same, humming tunelessly and feigning the quiet relish of a nicotine addict, even if I do feel as if I've just had a wisdom tooth packed with cotton. Suddenly, juices start to pour hot as acid from the tobacco leaves. Pepper and brimstone wash across my tongue. Navor and Juan look calm and untroubled, Russell indifferent, and yet he seems to be watching out of the corner of his eye. It's no good; I can't hold out any longer and, leaning to the far side of my horse, loudly and unceremoniously spit, as tears just start to melt my eyeliner.

"You guys must be hard-mouthed as a bad horse." I pick a black flake of tobacco from my lip, and unwrap a cool healing piece of peppermint gum that's nearly fused with its wrapper from the heat and, as they smirk, I suck out every trace of its flavor. No way could they chew such infernos so calmly. Did they slip me a bit of doctored weed, I wonder. And yet, they're plenty used to the seeded frenzy of chili peppers. Maybe they *are* like hard-mouthed horses now and barely notice the cutting edge of the bit.

When all the cows are safely grazing in high pasture, we turn lazily around and retrace our steps. Overhead, an eagle profits from an updraft, scouting the slopes as it veers across the sky. Stretching my arm, I separate the fingers till they look fringed as the eagle's wing. His bald head I know is for cleanliness' sake: less gore trapped when he pulls his head from a carcass. Thinking of all the ornithopter attempts, I have to laugh; a bird's wing flaps with such complex sweeps and puckers, and the bones are so hollow, the drag so little. A sudden gust, and he is off even before he knows it, flying as uncritically as a rock falls. But seeing butterflies and gnats fly gamely, with trim inexhaustible ease, just before the lift-off of *Viking II*, which needed a million or so pounds of fuel to launch it, was nearly more than I could bear. In the foreground, insects tootled among the grasses. And in the background the spacecraft strained on the pad, orange fire whooshing all around it as it suffered to move a meager yard or two, finally rising on a sea of flames and lumbering slowly into the cloudbanks, as birds gathered on the marshes. The irony hurt like a brush burn.

When I ask Navor what he thought of the last launch, he shakes his head and scowls.

"I saw the moon-walk," he said, "but I don't believe any of it. I think they do it in Hollywood, on one of those big lots where they make movies."

The sound of loudly falling raindrops distracts me and, turning round, I'm just in time to see Mettie, a horse-length away, riding up at full gallop. He grabs my horse's tail and tries to ride off with it; Roany panics, I scream. Then Mettie, fidgeting his horse's rump, brings on a flurry of kicks at

Roany's nose and belly. How, I have no idea, but he signals his horse to do a hip-swaying two-step of bucks, then leap straight into a big mud puddle in front of us, buck again, and splatter me head to toe.

"Mettie!" I scream venomously, shattered by the frustration of not knowing how to retaliate. I light out after him, but stop short a few strides later, puzzled by what I could do to him even if I could catch him. I sulk ostentatiously, and brush away the mud, muttering with rage, as Mettie, Terry, and Don canter on to headquarters.

14

Sunday morning, I wake at 5:00, as usual, fifteen minutes before the alarms, even though I went to sleep at 10:00, with visions of prairie dancing like sugarplums in my head. I put on a pair of pants and a bright-yellow shirt. I will be the sun. I will be the low clumps of yellow flowers that sit in the dirt like bouquets. I will be the ever-present sunflowers blowing in the light winds of *madrugada* (early morning): a circle of black hair haloed in yellow.

At 5:50, it's a cool, clear day, the air mountain-fresh as I make my way to the cookhouse. The ranch is silent as a pyramid. No lights. No movement. Mettie's black truck sits next to Rachel's at her trailer. Late from Logan, he must have spent the night there. I sit on the barbed-wire fence for some time, just contemplating the murky vista, and watching the ranch sleep as if it were a lover. Finally, I stroll to the cookhouse where, oddly, it's still dark throughout. Even the insects seem quieter. The whole ranch must sleep late on Sundays.

Ah, well, I walk back to the school and put on yesterday's pot of ropy black coffee. The sun rises at 6:30, as if it's been lassoed and dragged kicking and bawling into the day; by noon it will roar on the mesas. By late afternoon, Lynda, Terry, Don, and I will have swum in the creek and picnicked near the ghost town of Albert, trucking our horses part way and riding the rest. Sherrie and I are not built alike; in her swimsuit, I both bulge and slosh.

A clutch of hefty rocks stand slabwise on top of a mesa, as if they have been fused there by some heavenly rage. How Christianity flourished, in a landscape that looks as if it's been toyed with by a roomful of malicious gods, I've no idea. What drama—rocks ripped open and chunked, carved, battered, sandblasted, and gutted—all by wind and water.

"Huh?" Lynda wrinkles her face, as she puzzles over my remark that the landscape is "dramatic."

"What does that mean?" she asks about a land as familiar to her as my backyard is to me.

"I mean that it looks like a lot happened here, like things, moving very hard and fast once, were tossed up and spun around and came to rest where they are now. . . . Imagine a play in which people keep running and jumping across the stage. To me, it looks like, on the stage of this land, rocks have been leaping and rolling: moving like dancers. And over there like pigs wallowing in mud. And over there like doors being slammed in a cloud's face."

"Whew." Lynda shakes her head indulgently. A crazy person is riding with her, a person who thinks of these old bare rocks as dancers.

By dinnertime, Delois has made sun-brewed tea, by putting a jug full of cold water and teabags out in the blistering sun. Russell says you wouldn't think it could make such a difference, but it does. This year again Delois has won a prize at the flower show that's part of the local county fair. One day, driving to town, she confesses she's got a yen to learn how to belly-dance.

Sitting outside the bunkhouse, on its cement porch, with Lynda, Rachel, and the cowboys, I watch Delois quick-step to the cookhouse and offices where Russell will be working. An urgent message, perhaps, but it looks more like a fight's in store. Taking a sharp piece of chalklike rock, I write LUNA, a Spanish reference to my name, on the cement.

"What's that?" Lynda scrunches her face.

When I explain about Diana being the goddess of the moon, she starts to giggle uncontrollably.

"That's not what we call you—"

Rachel shushes her, and starts to giggle herself.

"What *do* you call me?"

The cowboys tilt their hats down to hide their smiles.

"Come on, what do you all call me?" I ask fearing the worst.

"Well . . . haven't you heard Susie calling you it?" Lynda asks incredulously.

"Yes, something. But what?"

Exchanged glances embolden her. She looks from face to face for a signal to keep quiet and, finding none, blurts: "We call you *Wonderwoman!*"

Rachel claps her hands as she laughs. And I look less like a super-heroine than a made-up hyena, as I cackle more loudly than anyone. Susie's "Wunnerwoo!" Now it makes sense. The hair, Lynda explains, and my constant bustle. And Wonder-woman's real name being Diana something-or-other. And my flashy duds (seeing the fire-engine red, pointy-toed western boots, Lynda had said politely, "They sure go nicely with your purple chaps"). Mostly the hair, which recently was cut into a cross between Cardinal Richelieu's and a Parisian whore's, but now is growing out thick and sky high. Wonderwoman, indeed; I feel more like a refugee from a cartoon by Gahan Wilson.

"Hey, Susie," I say as we all go in for dinner, "who am I? Who am I?"

Susie grins till her dimples form.

"Who am I?"

Like a rooster warming up for the crow, she stretches her tiny neck and says, "Wunnerwoo!"

For the third day in a row, we horn brand the cows, driving them into glossy, green, squeeze shoots, slamming the head-stalls closed around their necks, tying their heads (and horns) safely back with the help of a "twitch" (metal pliers-grip) on their noses, burning identification numbers into each horn, and painting the numbers with bright-red enamel. Again, all the animals are sprayed for flies, and carefully checked for pinkeye and other ailments. Never will they enter the squeeze shoot without a fuss. Don hangs on the shoot lever, ready to drop all his weight the instant a cow is in place, when the bars will spring closed like a venus-flytrap's cage, gripping the startled animal. Twitch in hand, Russell waits just out of sight. But Juan's job is the messiest: prodding the cows through the warrens, cranking their tails and shoving his shoulder against half tons of obstinate beef. Splattered with green feces, he just misses the rapier jab of a horn by leaping onto a high fence rail and conducting traffic with his feet. Down he jumps again into the crud, to haze another panicky cow through the shoot. My job's a snap. First I fill two syringes with medicine, just as R. J. once taught me in the branding corral, and hand them, one at a time, to Russell, who carefully treats the occasional case of pinkeye. Then, with a paintbrush small enough to do logos on a model plane, I fill each of Russell's freshly branded horn numbers with red paint, while he burns numbers into the second horn. So much hubbub, smoke, odor, and springing muscles is there, it hardly seems the time to explain about my adrenal problem, which causes me very little trouble these days—except that my hands, even in calm moments, always tremble just a smidgen. Make me nervous and they quake like the wreck of the *Hesperus*.

Setting the paint can on the table, I take aim at the clear, burnished numbers on one horn (which look finely tooled as the LATHAM tooled into Russell's belt), and end up polka-dotting everything in sight.

"How about a Cheshire cat?"

Russell isn't amused.

"Be easier to identify."

"Get it in the number," he says calmly, and shows me how to meticulously paint an *8*. No splatter, no trickles, no smudge. He cares. It's a minor work of art.

The cow is restless, and starting to twitch from its "twitch," so I redip my brush and try again, ducking the sharp stab of each horn. This time I brace my painting elbow against my side, and hold the wrist steady with my free hand. My gum I've begun to chew with open-mouthed abandon. A *3*, an *8*: who's to say? Russell's eyes close wearily; he is not going to yell, but it will not do. A cowboy would have to dismount to see what number the cow was. I wipe away what extraneous red flourishes I can, and pray my next cow horn will be tidier, in vain.

In the cookhouse bathroom, I find a large bottle of Jergen's lotion, just as I do all over the ranch, and am grateful. Most of the red paint comes off with nail-polish remover, but it takes a pot scrubber's devotion, and even then speckles remain. Eating, we look like a chain gang with the pox.

"I see you've got Prince saddled," Mettie says, as he sits down.

"Yes, but the cinch isn't fastened."

"The saddle is backwards." He pours some gut-ripping chili sauce over his potatoes and beans.

"What do you mean *backwards*?" I ask.

"The saddle horn, it's underneath."

"What?! Mettie, how could you?"

"Not me," he says, as he might to a McCarthy-era inquest. "The horse did it."

"The horse took off his saddle and buckled both cinches on his back?"

"I don't know; that's how it is." He presses a slice of bread into the chili sauce until it changes color.

"Sigh," I lament, "it's not even past noon, and already you guys are starting in on me."

"No," Mettie says, looking wrongly accused, "not me."

Out in the barn I find a bewildered Prince, his saddle hanging horn-down under his belly, both cinches buckled securely on his back. I'm not sure I even know how Mettie managed to lift the saddle up to fasten it.

Siesta time passes quickly, and though I'm tempted to go out with Mettie and Terry to spread salt, I decide to give them their privacy again, and paint some more cattle with Russell. At the corral, I find Terry, Juan, Russell, and Mettie huddled over the open hood of Mettie's new pickup, checking the parts as if they were reading the entrails of a hawk.

"What would you prefer," I ask Terry quietly, "if I went with you guys, or stayed and worked with Russell?" Terry says he doesn't care; Mettie says, really, it doesn't matter.

"You guys want to bum around alone?" I ask Mettie in a whisper.

"No," he says, "whatever."

So I hop into the truck between them, toss my purple chaps on the dashboard, and off we zoom to throw salt and minerals in each of the troughs near the waterholes. Terry begins to grin mischievously before we even cross the cattle guard, and, seeing headquarters disappear behind us, it occurs to me that this might not have been the best choice.

From the glove compartment, Mettie pulls a pouch of Red Man chewing tobacco, and offers me some.

"Listen, bunkie, I've been this route three times now. How often can one woman fall for the same gag?"

"No," Mettie assures me in his honest-as-the-day-is-long voice, "this isn't like snuff. Not like Russell's tobacco either. The others, they were teasing you."

Terry's grin looks molded in wax, eternal, the god of mischief come to life in a pickup truck.

Driving one-handed in and out of mud trenches, Mettie gives the truck its head as he would a stumbling horse. In the other hand, he still holds the pouch of tobacco. His knuckles, I notice, are tattooed with his name.

"Okay. What do I do?"

He shows me how to take a wad of tobacco between my fingers, roll it into a ball, and pack it into my cheek. Brown, gooey saliva geysers instantly, but the taste isn't bad, a little like Raisin Bran cereal in fact, with a sweet, damp aroma.

"What do I do with the juice?" I ask, barely able to speak without dribbling. The strange bulge in my cheek I stroke lightly; it reminds me of pre-Columbian terra-cottas of men whose cheek bulges were filled with cocaine.

"Swallow it," he says. "I do."

For a while, I do swallow it, but the juices grow progressively randier, thicker.

"My god, you could plant corn in it!" I complain, and take to spitting little brown comets out the window, past Terry, or larger ones when he obligingly opens the door. Soon my head starts to cloud and get woozy, and, though it amuses the deadly duo no end, I finally follow the yearnings of my stomach and spit the tobacco into a cushion of sagebrush.

Apparently, they've decided to make my last day memorable; without so much as time out to cabal, they ad lib a two-man siege and, for the next five hours, dive-bomb me like hornets. They lock me out of the truck. To retaliate, I take the black masking tape from the glove compartment and tape all of the dashboard knobs closed. They steal my chaps; I steal their hats and gloves. They make wry insinuations. I get out my lipstick and threaten to feminize them. After spreading gritty minerals, they make me roll up the bags so that salt dust will coat my mouth and nose. I stuff empty bags into one large one, and clobber them with it. Finding a bull snake in the road, Terry lifts it over a broom handle and wags it at me; when I run back to the truck, I find Mettie inside whistling, all the doors locked. I put one of Terry's work gloves to my mouth, inflate it, and get ready to pop it like a balloon. They threaten to drag my chaps in the creekbed, along the barbed wire, under a cattle guard.

"Terry, if you don't give me my chaps back," I yell, "I'm going to forget that I'm a lady."

Separating them at the belt, he now has two prizes to work with, each one purple as a hyacinth; one of them he flings out of the truck window. I follow up by tossing out a green-and-white cap. Mettie slams on the brakes, and Terry and I race down the highway, just as a passing semi whizzes by, its driver perplexed by the road-shoulder shenanigans. Each time Terry leaps from the truck to open a pasture gate, I lock his door. He snatches my chaps for the twentieth or thirtieth time and, as I lunge after a pair of gloves to use as barter, Mettie jumps clear and opens the door, out of which I tumble into the sand, head first, my legs macabrely twisted around the seat. *Patas arriba.* They are monsters.

"Take heart," Terry urges as we drive back to headquarters, "you've got five months to dream up your revenge."

At the last gate, I again lock Terry out, but this time he seems to be hiding something behind his back. Inside the truck, he brings cupped hands around front with a wicked grin. Then I remember how yesterday, in the shipping pen, he'd held cupped hands under my nose and asked if I wanted a peek. At my "yes," his hands opened and two fistfuls of black noisy flies mobbed my face. Now my eyes stretch wide with horror and, leaping off my seat, I cling to the roof of the truck. Mettie is screaming with laughter; I am just screaming.

* * *

"You look a trifle beat," Russell says, appraising the damage visible in face and clothes.

"Russell, I don't suppose I have to tell *you* this," I say, rolling my neck like a radar dish to ease its strained muscles, "but going out with the two of them is like a jackrabbit volunteering to go out with two coyotes."

He laughs out loud, and nods knowingly.

"God, do they really resent me that much?"

"Resent you?" Russell looks flabbergasted. "Why, that's their way of showing affection."

"Affection? What the hell do they do if they *don't* like you?"

"Ignore you."

Whistling a bird-twittery movie theme, I walk through mud and large, deep puddles down the road, my truck left safely at the Mitchells'. Often I stop along the way to admire the sunset—salmon and blue—on which sheet lightning explodes like the artillery of a distant war. Someone begins to mimic me and yet, spinning around, I find no one in sight. I whistle again, tentatively, then more loudly, and laugh when I realize what's happening: an echo. "Echo!" I call. And "Echo!" my voice hurls back from the ring of scarlet mesas.

At dinner, with the fried steak, home fries, squash and corn, beans, bread and butter, and big bowlfuls of fruited Jell-O, Mettie gives me a green pepper to try in its natural state. Does the tenderfoot have a tender mouth? Absolutely, so I begin at the safe, pointy end of the pepper, surprised by its mild flavor. Inside, white seeds cling to the pepper's ribs like tiny organs. With the tip of my tongue, I lick one of them, and my sinuses explode.

"*¡Muy caliente!*"

"No," Mettie says, "you must eat all the seeds, all of them to be a cowboy."

White lightning. The Inquisition was kinder. It occurs to

me that I ought not to waste such a diabolical effort.

"If I eat the whole thing," I ask slyly, "can I ride one of your palominos?"

Everyone stops eating. Mettie agrees, but only if I eat all of the seeds.

"Promise?" I demand, eyeing the pepper, its white seeds like flywheels, its green stem trembling between my fingers. Can you die from chili pepper burn? Probably not, though I suspect, gums a-flame, one might wish to.

"*Sí,* I promise," he says, "now eat."

Juan hides his eyes and howling grin with one hand, not needing to actually witness the carnage. Adelina giggles at the other end of the table, her daughter's eyes widening. Don shakes his head wearily.

"See what a woman will do to ride a beautiful horse," I say, hesitating for the last possible second to savor the normal state of my senses, then pop the entire cob of vitriolic seeds into my mouth and, tears welling up, swallow it in two chunks. I know better than to chew it. What feels like nerve gas roars through my throat, scratches and smokes; then needles prick my tongue, scarify my gums; and, finally, even my lips feel scalded. Tears make wide arroyos down my cheek. Have I swallowed the last of the pepper? So volcanic is my throat, I can't tell whether it's throbbing because the seeds are still in it or have gone by. Adelina puts a glass of iced tea in front of me, and I need no coaxing to gargle with it, or ask for a refill, while she twitches with laughter.

"You promised," I whisper huskily to Mettie.

"Okay," he concedes, "next time you come, you can ride Popcorn. I'll gentle him down for you."

My tongue actually hurts, feels bruised, pin-cushiony, and hot, so the first chance I get I head for the bathroom and hang it under the cold tap water like a pelt.

15

Though my tongue has recovered, my arms and legs ache as if they have been the focus of a torture squad. Bruises the size of silver dollars ornament my thighs, one of them darker and redder-purple than a sunset. Gimpy, I stumble to the truck and drive sleepily to breakfast. Mettie is finishing up his first three eggs; he fries up three more.

"I thought you were kidding about eating six eggs for breakfast," I say, buttering a slice of toast.

"No, told you I wasn't joking."

"They must have to keep a chicken just for you."

"Probably."

Mettie looks sleepy this morning. None of the other cowboys have shown up, even though it's well past six. None of the horses have been wrangled yet either. Yesterday was so exhausting, even by ranch standards, that today a little toe-dragging won't be condemned. Mettie notes that he tossed and turned all night.

"Jactitating," I say mechanically.

Looking up from his second trinity of eggs, his eyes loiter in the air. "Haven't done that since I was fourteen," he says finally.

"No, no, no," I erase the air with one hand, "not *that* word. Hair doesn't grow on your palms."

"Yes, white hair; our mothers tell us the same thing." He grins. Some things are universal.

"No, no, the word I said was *jactitating*. It means to toss and turn . . . I swear . . . *really*."

Mettie shakes his head, and goes to pour the first of his several glasses of milk. Coffee is not on his menu. The other cowboys will eat fabulous amounts of pure protein, too, and by lunchtime have burned up every trace of it, their bodies efficient as dynamos. I give my dishes to Adelina, and trot outside for a last look around the corrals flooded with rainwater and apricot light. Mettie's truck, as usual, is parked next to the bunkhouse. Quietly opening its door, I turn the windshield wipers on, the heat and radio up full, so that later, when I'm gone and he starts the ignition, the truck will come to life like a booby trap.

Al whistles tunefully as we taxi along the airstrip. For the first time in weeks, I don't hear the cicadas rasping in the roadside curtains of wild sunflowers. Up we float, smoothly, in a wide semi-circle, as Al climbs toward the mesas, then banks the plane back over headquarters and levels out for a moment. My feet, on the training pedals, follow his; my jittery hands get ready to take the controls.

"Look," he says, suddenly pointing far below us to where two cars sit, bumper to bumper, at the main gate. Beside them stand Sherrie and Lynda (headed for ballet lessons in Tucumcari) and Tom (sent to rescue their mud-mired car). Al dives steeply and buzzes them to say hello, then, with a grin, he shoots straight up at such speed I flatten against the seat, the air punched out of me.

Prying my head loose, I watch him swim with laughter, in his eyes an unmistakable *Gotcha*! One more sweep over headquarters, and we are off to Amarillo; behind us the corral, bunkhouse, and other buildings dwindle to points of light. Tomorrow they'll seem as far away as quasars.

Preface to Part III

Flying to Pasadena last week, I read a hyped-up paperback about women of the Old West, and tensed between shivers and flushes as I learned about mission women being raped and tortured by Indians, floozies winning the hearts (and purses) of gold-rush miners, homestead women breaking sod from dawn to dusk, lady sharpshooters, derelicts, desperadoes, legendary sybarites such as Colonel Custer's wife (who insisted on bathing every morning, even if, as often, they were on maneuvers), schoolmarms, reformers, and kidnapped women of letters who returned to write about their concubinage among the Apaches or Utes, not to mention the more ordinary women of the wagon trains whose piecemeal agonies were commemorated by fresh graves every fifty miles.

I glanced out of the tiny porthole, to rest my eyes and recover a little from the emotional free-for-all, and there were the Rockies, like alligator hides stretched below, enormous even from our altitude, and disappearing only at the horizon. Slow motion, we wind-galloped over them. How did the pioneers ever cross such endless, towering mountains with nothing but yoked oxen and wooden-wheeled Conestogas? Then, as if a rash had abruptly healed, the mountains stopped and desert loomed unbroken to L.A.

Fate plays few tricks so telescopically right as to carry me to the Jet Propulsion Laboratory, to watch the first close-ups of Jupiter pour in, the same week I'm due back on the Tequesquite. All night, we sat in taupe, card-table chairs that did nothing to rest that rise of muscles shaking hands around one's spine: too exhausted to speak, and too full of wonder to go home to bed. Every now and then somebody got up and shuffled to the buffet laid out thoughtfully in the back of the room, keeping eyes fixed on the TV screen and, between swipes at his bread with a mustard-clotted knife, turning around to make sure he didn't miss a new frame. Io flashed on the screen like a ball of golden gunshot. Often my favorite part of Jupiter appeared: the flouncy white swirls around the Red Spot, which reminded one commentator of "surf breaking on a shore," but to me looks more like the hem of a flamenco skirt—soft petticoats furling and swaying to a tune lively as Creation.

What a world: in one week to cross the Rockies, see television from Jupiter, and return to cowboying. My time frame's all a-jumble. Dipsochronicity. On Io there are salt flats like those in Arizona. Jupiter, of course, is gaily striped, but so are the mesas which may tell us just as much about how the solar system began. One day we'll know, and I hope someone will come back and tell me. But meanwhile I'll pack my bags for tomorrow's journey to a spot a little closer to home.

Over Christmas, I scuba-dived among the Bahamian reefs, thinking hard about our lobe-fish ancestors, and feeling a part of the element that gave birth to us all. Last month, I spent two of the longest minutes I can recollect in a doctor's office, watching a machine tremble a small card whose chemical flux would tell if I were pregnant. And now Jupiter, which we hope will say something astounding about the swirling placenta from which all the planets came. Which is only to say that wombs have been on my mind a lot lately.

A timely call from Al Mitchell tells me that calving season is well under way. Seventy calves have already dropped, and it's only early March. Another 300 await my arrival. But the conversation is one way, so poor is the connection between Ithaca and Mosquero, Mosquero and the ranch. He hears me well enough, but *his* voice comes through in shards, every other syllable missing. I try at least to picture him, at the cluttered captain's desk, in the office whose bookshelves are heaped high with a wide array of popular titles, coffee-table books, modern classics, and westiana. Now the copy of Antoine de Saint-Exupéry's flight journal, *Wind, Sand and Stars*, which I recently sent, will be there, too, among books by Hemingway and Dag Hammarskjöld.

"Should I bring something warm to wear?" I ask.

"Washable," he answers, his drawl giving the word just enough syllables for me to make sense of it. My pulse pounds hard when I imagine what gynecological mayhem that one-word answer suggests.

PART III

Calving Season

March

16

In the velour coziness of the Chicago airport lounge, I recheck my camera and cartridge-belt of film, letting imagination stage the reunion to come in six or seven hours. A car rented in Amarillo will carry me through the scenic nowhere of West Texas to the border town of Glen Rio (as large as its one bar), then Logan, which is big city compared to the populationless sprawl that surrounds it, and halfway to Mosquero before I turn onto the weatherbeaten ranch road I've come to know so well. Someone standing close by startles me, softly calling my name. I track the long, blue-jeaned legs up to the face that tops them: Terry Mitchell on his way home from school, looking just as I remember him, but two heads taller. And something in the way his face relaxes tells me that he has grown in other ways, too. Is the change from sixteen to seventeen always this dramatic? Perhaps it's the term he and a handful of boys from Deerfield Academy just spent at an all-girls school in Troy, New York. That would rev up any boy's tachometer. Terry explains that his dad will be fetching us in Amarillo, having guessed our flights might overlap. On flight paths, the Northeast meets the Southwest infrequently, and rarely without the buffer stop of Chicago. Nor is it any coincidence time goes backward as we progress, over Wichita cornfields down into the cattle-crop country.

Although the Tequesquite's orange-and-white Beechcraft puts it in touch with the outside world, "going to town" is still a luxury. Al has saved up his errands, the first of which is greeting us, a gray felt Stetson hat in hand, with a cowboy's suntan and a wide-brimmed smile. Once we load Terry's caravan of suitcases, skis, laundry, and other fare, we drop him off at the doctor's for a check-up, since he's been exposed to mononucleosis at school, and set off for the day's town chores. At the electrician's, Al picks up three drills of various sizes and bit-shapes, which have been enlivened by new cords, while the shopkeeper eyes me cagily ("Probably thinks you're a second wife," Al whispers). Next stop is the rancher's supermarket: a large, two-building hardware store, where a girl takes his order for windmill parts, shovel handles (just handles, no blades), pipes, and sundry fittings. Outside it's 40° F and windy—no season to be fixing windmills in.

The stock girl asks to whom to bill the goods.

"T. E. Mitchell and Son, Inc., Albert, New Mexico," Al answers, while she riffles through a drawer of charge folders. She pulls out his account, and jots down the new charges.

"Don't get many folks from Albert," she says.

Al winks, and I wonder if he is going to tell her that his ranch *is* the population of Albert. But no, the gag is too good to spoil; he'll keep mum, and one day, many trips from now, it will finally dawn on her.

A quick stop at the small appliance-repair shop gets us a newly mended electric razor. The streets of Amarillo are just as sprawly and single story as Pasadena, but much cleaner and windswept. A light breeze keeps litter and dust on the move, and it's easy to picture turn-of-the-century life with hitching posts and little snarls of tumbleweed. Terry, it turns out, is run down but undiseased. I welcome him to the afflictions of academic life. Over lunch, we discuss his future college, Texas A & M, where Tom is already a freshman. Al is keen on all of his boys having a master's degree of one sort or another; years ago, a B.A. in agriculture would have been plenty.

Between swigs of iced tea, Al fills me in on the recent changes in personnel. What a turnover! Mike left, though it's hard to say why. When he returned from the hospital, after an arm injury, he was just a different man; it was as if he had suddenly discovered his mortality. Within a few weeks, he had tossed his saddle into his pickup truck, said goodbye to no one, and left behind him only a long wake of dust. Becky, the new schoolmarm, a blonde, pleasant-featured girl from Massachusetts, had arrived with her car, her books, and her worldly possessions to take root on the ranch like one of the imported jonquils. Russell and his family had left, to go into the windmill business. The next jigsaw piece falling away was one they all expected: Don pulled out just after the Lathams, stayed with them a short spell in Logan, and moved back to his home state, Kansas, to manage a horse ranch. Russell had been a "foreman." His replacement, Wallace Cox, whom Al seems tickled a hundred ways to have found, is "assistant manager," and a topflight, well-educated man with long experience working for the state. To replace Don, Wallace suggested a young farm boy from Deming, New Mexico, Steve Allen. "Ah, yes," Al smiles as he tells me about the latest addition to the ranch family: Adelina's new baby, "Angelica."

After lunch, father and son get their hair washed and cut. Al dozes in the chair, while the barber dries his hair with a blowgun, the spot-heat easing muscles at his neck and temples. A shoeshine man squats by Terry's feet, daubs a bit of polish onto his freckled boots and buffs them to a high, military gloss by swinging the rag back and forth across the boots with the long steady rhythm of a violinist.

Today is Tom Mitchell's birthday, so our last stop is an office-supply store, where we inspect a wardrobe of calculators, each sleeker and more intelligent than the last. Already, in my own lifetime, slide rules have become antiques. I remember high-school boys loitering in the hallways, fidgeting with their slide rules which, when not in use, dangled from their belts like swords. In symposia or lectures, out came Excalibur, with the audience forever gliding plastic back and forth to follow the calculations of the speaker. Now audiences touch miniaturized machines so discreetly you wonder if they're not just doing palmistry, or itching. Terry puts the most complex calculator through its paces, and pronounces it omnicompetent.

At last it's time to go to the airport, where Al drives straight up to the right wing of his plane, unloads our gear into the hold, and drops off his rented car nearby. In a few minutes, we are airborne, returning to the ranch by the scenic route, low over the ground. Stark, flat, sprawling, until only the horizon can stop it, the land looks brawny and desolate. Those used to the security of mountains, like bolsters holding all of life close around them, might find it unsettling to live in such emptiness. I find it liberating, as if the universe began here in a flywheel of winds, sage, sand, and color, moving from the spore-packed dust close at hand to the shifting blues of the horizon and the thinning ethers far beyond. Al points to two kinds of soil below us: one that's baked hard and tight, and another, sandier, soil he prefers for grazing cattle. In the looser soil grow dense clumps of sage and yucca. A flash in the cloud, a twinkle, he spots as a plane. And soon enough it becomes clear that he is seeing much more than I am. Speckles of white, like dewdrops or first crocuses, are antelope running wild in a ravine. Speckles of black like a shake of coarse pepper are Black Angus steers. Red and white stripes in the distance are a watchtower. An insect with a rectangular carapace is a truck. The higher we climb, the more my senses kaleidoscope. Clumps of sagebrush seem only twenty feet below us. Suddenly, a pickup truck appears, small as an ingot, and I telescope my bewildered sight to a new focus. But in no time the relativistic shimmy returns: the landscape is just too monotonous and unsettled to give easy yardsticks to an unseasoned eye. It could be the sea or the Arctic we are scouting without altimeter, and, at night, instruments must be all that holds one to life.

Out of the right-hand window, a homestead ringed in tall trees rolls into view. "It's a pretty ranch, isn't it?" Al halts his whistling to say, meaning that where there are so few trees, what pretties up a ranch is its lovely ring of shade. With no other buildings or trees to be seen in any direction, the ranch looks staked out against the elements, planned, cozy, an oasis, a dike against the ravages of wind and spirit.

Soon dark hills, huddled like rug merchants, appear in the middle of the prairie, and mark the eastern boundary of the Tequesquite. We circle the headquarters once, then Al tips a wing hard on my side to give me a good view of the buildings skidding out below us like skaters on a whip. I want to tell him that, tilted on one side like this, while the ranch world rotates, I feel like the North Wind on ancient maps, his cheeks puffed full as he invigilates the comings and goings of the world. But now Al levels out fast, drops swiftly onto the landing strip, furrowed from many landings, snowmelt, and mud, and sets down smoothly, not far from a herd of cows who stop grazing to eye us. No threat, they decide, but just in case, they stand stiff and alert until we taxi well past them and on to the hangar, with Al trying to keep as little pressure on the front wheel as human effort and the gouged road permit. On cue, a gold pickup truck turns down the airstrip road and bounces toward us.

"Whose rig? Yours with Rachel?" I ask, but see two people

in the truck, one full-sized driver at the wheel, and a small head poking up over the dashboard. Recognizing Lynda, Al smiles. Soon a green pickup appears for the welcome, too, with Sherrie at the wheel, slimmer and blue-jeaned, hair cut into a short, smart style, and eyes full of welcome. A big-eye tyke on the bench-seat beside her, Susie has not grown much in the last few months, but she is all jabber. Her eyes open wide at my black hair that probably looks like something she last saw at Halloween.

"Want to see the baby?" she pleads, yanking my hand. "Want to see Adelina? Want to see my porch?"

The porch? I ask Sherrie, "There's a new porch on the cookhouse?" Sherrie closes her eyes and shakes her head no.

Last time I saw Susie she was at the tail end of the terrible twos; now she's full speed ahead into the talkative threes. "She's just excited to see company, but let's go to the cookhouse anyway," Sherrie says, and slides back into the truck. Susie stands on the seat between us, a hand on each of our shoulders, as she tells us breathlessly about the baby and Adelina and Juan and the porch and the digging (sewer repair) and again the baby, with each topic growing more and more pleased about her new menagerie of words. Things have names, and the discovery clearly thrills her. She can quiz people about what they're doing and thinking, offer testimonials, make jokes, describe life's whirlwinds and hubbubs. So new to fluent language, she is wonder-struck that it works. Each sentence is a new adventure, and her dark little heartbreaker eyes romp as she chats about the baby, who sits with toys in a modern crib, bewildered as a startled fawn, while mommy cooks and the grownups utter their strange noises. Susie's small hand pleads with mine so soulfully, I finally agree to stroll with her, and, yes, have a look at her "porch," whose secret has begun to intrigue me. Through the impressionist blur of the screen door, nothing looks different: cement floor, brown pipe pillars, window that catches the sun at rare angles, spreading light like wet frosting or oil slicks. But, in one corner, over a blue plastic swimming pool and tricycle, enormous cascades of red peppers, sewn carefully together, are drying in the sun, each bunch larger than Susie; her cheeks flush with a child's rapture for the extreme, the monstrous, or the overflowing. All that *red,* her face says. I know these peppers, like those I saw in Aunt Betty's kitchen, must be real, but again my hand moves instinctively to touch them to make sure they're not embers bunched on a rope, or red fire kelp, or *papier mâché.* "Mmmm, they're beautiful," is all I say, but Susie smiles to see how well I like her porch.

After dinner, Tom unwraps his presents, and soon the ranch members drift in to celebrate along with us, and share the rounds of birthday cake, ice cream, and pink champagne. Tom's newly shaven head (*de rigueur* for members of Texas A & M's paramilitary Honor Guard) is hard to get used to: it makes him look like a member of a Hare Krishna sect.

"Put on the guy with the curly red chest-hairs," Rachel calls, and a moment later Andy Gibb begins a mellow, syncopated disco tune about how he's just "a puppet on a string."

Juan sits quietly on a chair, balancing a plate of cake and ice cream on one knee, his fancy-stitched black boots with tall, underslung heels looking out of place gripping chair wood instead of stirrups. Wallace slides into the room, takes off his peaked cap, and holds it in front of him as Al introduces us. He passes his hat to one hand as we shake hands, and his smile is just as firm as his grip. From the deep suntan, I know he's been working hard for some months now, and his long fingers feel toughened from cold weather and wet work. If possible, he is even more handsome than Russell was, with the same blue eyes, but a bonier face, and a rougher, manlier complexion. But mostly Wallace is tall, almost tall enough to catch his hat on the lintel as he enters a room, and I'm sure he ducks low when he gets into the cab of a truck. But somehow the geography of his body works so well—long legs, slim hips, plateau chest, jutting cheekbones—he cuts a tall, wiry figure.

"You're so *big,* Wallace," Susie says, unable to restrain herself, "you're *sooo* big."

"Sure am," he says, laughing, and sits down beside her on the ledge of the bar, so she can see the face on top of all that leg.

Al introduces a young cowboy, with a head full of curly blond hair, as Steve Allen, the newest bunkhouse hand. Steve nods hello, hat in hand, dropping in a "M'am," as if it were a subway token. His pale cheeks make it clear that he's new to the ranch. I pity him his initiation, knowing as I do what it means to be low man on the totem pole. Twice already he's managed my trick of forgetting to unbuckle the back girth, and letting the horse run off with an expensive saddle dragging underneath, and three times he's been bucked off one of the horses in his remuda. Because he has so much hair, his hat won't stay on when he gallops and, because the curls are so luxurious and blond, the boys insist on calling him "Farrah Fawcett." Because he's so young, he's the brunt of sexual jokes, too. Al tells me on the quiet that he rolls well with the teasing, is high spirited and long suffering.

Party talk focuses on the day's calving: which cows have borne young without trouble, which pastures seem fullest at the moment, and then, amid head-shaking all around, the long list of difficult deliveries and stillborns. With fifty calves on their feet, calving season is well under way, but each ride the cowboys find cows that, for one reason or another, can't manage a natural birth. Usually, it's the young heifers, bearing a first calf, that find the going toughest. Try as they may, sometimes they'll push the calf no farther than the pelvic bone, where the pressure on its head and neck begin to choke it. Then the cowboys rush the heifer to cover, tie her horns to a fence, and feel inside to see how the calf is positioned.

If everything's right side up, they loop a chain around the calf's hooves, just above the fetlocks, and literally pull the calf out past the pelvic bone, winching the chain tighter and tighter, and dragging the newborn out by hand. Sometimes, of course, the calves arrive dead, or live only a short spell. For others, however, such impromptu midwifery works fine.

Already, there have been two cows with prolapsed wombs, which Wallace has had to jam back into place and stitch. Juan stands to show the posture of the calf he delivered this morning: one leg by its head and the other by its side, as if it were doing the Australian crawl. Somehow he managed to reach his hands in and turn the calf's wrong leg around, so it could be born correctly. Susie listens avidly, as he talks about his other babies, four legged, helpless, and even newer than her new sister, Angelica.

At night, in bed, I hear the steady heaving of the wind, howling and blowing as it does when it travels a long distance over the prairie. Yesterday, from home in Ithaca, I phoned the weatherman in Clayton, a small town in the northeast corner of New Mexico, to ask about the weather so I'd know what to pack. He was so tickled to be called all the way from New York, he recited every bit of weather he could find: rainfall, frost warnings, record highs and lows, and, as I wished, the last week's temperatures (60–67). I packed a spring dress and sandals along with my sweaters, old coat, and cossack hat, but the high in Albert today was 40^c. Now it's well below freezing, and tomorrow's riding in cold winds I can hear gathering from clear across the valley will make me feel shivery as the raw, wet calves we deliver. Snow still lies in patches far back on the mesas, but on the valley lands the grass is just beginning to turn taupe, on its way to lush blue-green. Shipping season had been torrid, hard-sweat weather, and branding season, in the dead of summer, even worse. Now, with cold and exposure in store, I consider how best to keep warm. Perhaps a pair of nylon stockings under my jeans to give me an extra thermal layer. Yes, that sounds good. Pulling the warm comforter close by my chin, I finally let the day go, and spiral into a deep, drugged sleep.

17

In the blue-black cascades of early morning, the wind howls from nowhere to nowhere; not even the tall grasses that, last trip, hid a bull snake from view and housed millions of fidgeting insects, have sprouted into the lush green to feed cattle and break the express winds. I imagine the moaning will stop at sunrise, but, in the darkness, my eyes water in sympathy, and I hurry to get dressed, out, and into whatever force is circling the trailer at such speed.

I pull a white, fake-fur hat of the cossack style down to my eyebrows and well over my ears, then zip a ski jacket over a turtleneck sweater, grab my chaps and gloves, and walk briskly through the just-brightening air, down the winding dirt road that leads to the cookhouse. Terrible deep trenches and tractor treads tell me how rough a winter the ranch has just had: snows, floods, mired pickup trucks, followed by a road grader trying to repair the damage.

One dog after another comes out to howl as I pass: Lyn's Trampus, Steve's calico mongrel Puder, Mettie's new black dog, which charges me in what I can see is well-rehearsed bluff.

"Easy, little wolf, I'm just passing through," I whisper, and crouch low, slapping one thigh as if to invite it to come play. It sneezes, and trots back to the bunkhouse. The other dogs, one by one, stop barking, and, by morning, presumably, they'll have forgotten the ghostly alarm.

In the cookhouse, Steve and Mettie have nearly finished breakfast.

"Hello, Wonderwoman," Mettie says, as he sponges up a bright egg yolk with a slice of toast. "How's New York?"

"Blizzard-struck. What a climate." My vocal cords, always sluggish to wake up, make me sound like Greta Garbo with a cold. For a moment, my sense of place deserts me; Mettie gets up when he sees me wandering gaga around the kitchen, plucks two eggs from a dish, and sets them in my hands as if they had been laid there.

"Thanks. I'm not awake," I explain needlessly.

He resumes breakfast by pouring a bowl of cereal, lifting his hand high to mix in the milk. The toast and strips of crunchy bacon, keeping warm at the back of the stove griddle, are for me. Turning the flame up under the bacon grease, I try to forget all the cholesterol propaganda, and crack two eggs into the sizzle.

"Have you met Farrah Fawcett yet?" Mettie says, nodding to Steve, whose luxurious blond hair curls into thick clusters. Steve blushes, trying to contain a smile between mouthfuls of bacon.

In the cast-iron frying pan, grease spits as I fiddle with the flame, and what's happening begins to dawn on me. *Steve* is now the tenderfoot, the pup, and *I'm* being offered a spot on the hazing line. I can't believe it. Gamely, I turn around to give his blond bundle a once-over, while a blush starts to cut across his cheeks again.

"You're right, that blond hair sure is pretty." I lift the eggs lightly, and flip them with a spatula, watching as they turn a sickening yellow. "Bet he's gonna' make someone a wonderful wife." At 6:00 A.M., wit comes hard.

Mettie smiles, and starts to pack a black lunchpail. He'll be packing an extra horse, as well, so many pastures does he have to check before nightfall. Steve rinses his dishes and heads for the corral to feed the colts, before saddling up for the day's work. Although I haven't had two consecutive hours of sleep, I down my breakfast and quickly follow, getting to the corral just as Juan appears, in his work clothes: chaps, cap, and a corduroy jacket into which he has stitched a complete down jacket for added warmth. I tell Juan to wrangle me one of Mettie's horses, that he said I could ride one. Juan knows better.

"He said you could ride his horse?" Juan asks, as if he'd just been told night would fall twice today.

"Well, it is true that he also said he would kill me if I did."

Juan laughs; that sounds more like Mettie. My old buddy, Prince, is grazing high on the mesa with some of the ranch's other horses, so this stay I'll be riding Crackerjack, a twenty-year-old chestnut gelding, and it occurs to me that I've never seen a twenty-year-old horse. I'm just wondering what a geriatric cutting horse looks like when, from across the yard, I hear a strange combination of sounds: pounding hooves, a motor, brakes squeaking, and round-up warbles. Leaping out of the way, as the first horse trots round the corner, I see, to my surprise, a bit of winter wrangling. Driving a pickup truck with one hand, Juan leans out of the window and flails the other hand to urge the horses on, moving the truck smoothly behind the herd just as he would a wrangling horse.

Hoofbeats work like a gong; the cowboys appear out of nowhere. Wallace, with his chaps hanging loose around his thin legs, adjusts the sit of his cap. His long body leans in the direction he's walking, and, before he enters the corral, he fastens the front of his brown vest. Steve comes straight from feeding the colts, dusting bits of hay from his coat and pants. Mettie emerges from the bunkhouse in the same red chaps I last saw him in, only now their original color is open to bet, most of the silver *conchas* are missing, and strange hieroglyphics spot the knees. He pulls a round-topped black felt hat down low on his head, as if to fix it in a permanent groove. Al appears in a pair of tie-dyed blue jeans, a pale western shirt, and a clean hat; but his chaps are worn shiny, dark, and full of splotches where each season has left its blood, sweat, medicine, and oil. Sleepy voices greet each other in the corral, as each cowboy ropes his morning horse. No one is quite awake. Soon Navor arrives with his morning horse, and Terry and Tom, sleepy eyed, but on their feet, are somnambulantly roping and saddling their horses.

A quick discussion decides I'll do morning rounds with Steve and Juan in their pasture, the West Bar-T, which henceforth will be my pasture, too. Steve is still smiling as we load our horses into the trailer. A quick trip to the medical refrigerator fetches antibiotics of various sorts, in case we run into trouble. Juan takes the wheel, I climb in next, and Steve, jumping in beside me, slaps on the truck door, calling for Puder to join us. A ball of calico leaps high over the tailgate and braces itself for the ride.

The West Bar-T is a nearby pasture, with shallow creekbeds winding like loose twine, deeper arroyos, several windmills pumping along the sprawly fence line, and a barn with six stalls and a small corral. A "Ditchwitch" stands ready in case graves are needed. Mettie recently killed a skunk in the barn, but the smell is gone now, replaced by the usual bouquet of cow and birth odors, straw, damp clay, and shade. I often wonder how shade can smell as distinctive as it does, as distinctive, in fact, as rain.

We untrailer our horses by reaching a hand through the bars and backing them out, one by one, grabbing the reins, as their front legs step to the ground. Checking my girth, I glance

Horn branding: my job is to paint the fresh numbers neatly with red, despite my hands' tendency to tremble.

Sun up: the corrals fill with apricot light. A beardless Mettie saddles up for his morning rounds.

Al and Navor fighting for the life of a newborn; as a last resort, they even drape the calf over a fence rail to force air into its lungs.

Adelina and Susie on the cookhouse porch.

Some of the hands ready to ride out for afternoon work. *From left to right:* Steve, Lyn, the author, Terry, Wallace, Mettie.

Lunch in the cookhouse. *From left to right:* Mettie, Terry, Tom, and Wallace.

Heifer with an orphan calf which has been wrapped in the skin of the heifer's dead calf so it will smell like her own.

Success. Al with a newborn that made it.

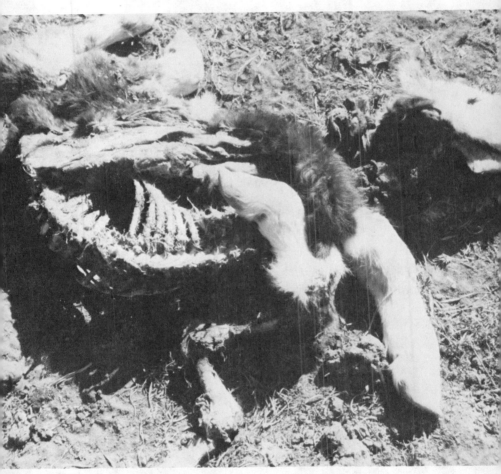

What the coyotes and crows leave. A painful sight I stumbled on in the West Bar T pasture.

Dawn of a workday.

With dog "Puder," Steve on his rounds, checking a heifer and newborn calf. On the horizon, Juan does the same.

over the saddle to see a gold pickup heading toward us, Al
coming at a fast clip from Navor's pasture. A squawk on the
two-way radio summons Juan. Trouble with one of the heifers
has reached a critical point, and he's just close enough to
fetch me to be on hand for the birth. Juan presses in the
button on the microphone head, and replies with a terse,
"Okay," turns Crackerjack free in the corral, and mounts up,
lifting an open hand in goodbye as he and Steve jog off
toward the creekbed. Puder scampers close by the horses'
heels, and I can see Steve tilt his hatrim down, glance back,
and smile, as Al pulls in, and I jump into the truck.

"What's up?"

Al shakes his head. "It doesn't look good," he drawls. "We
should have gotten to this heifer hours ago." On his dark face,
worry lines crab. "She must have gone into labor early this
morning. We needed to get to her hours ago."

Navor is waiting in the corral, with the bloated heifer tied
by her horns to a fence slat, while he gets out gynecological
gloves and birthing aids. I can see that Al is trying to be calm,
but he jumps out of the truck, slams the door, and opens the
corral gate without once taking his eyes off the heifer. A pale
sun is just starting to rise above the horizon, and, in the sky,
gray clouds bulk heavy as a comforter. Rain, we hope, not
just this suffocating cover. The red slats look like *terra-cotta*
in a gaining light that casts no shadows.

Al lifts a flesh-colored surgical glove out of a box, and slips
it on clear up to his shoulder. Another he gives me. Every few
seconds, the heifer tries to bear down, but by now, as we all
know, she won't be able to push the calf out by herself. From
trying for hours, she's exhausted and in shock. Navor men-
tions the calf's tongue, and Al begins to move with renewed
purpose. He puts his hand into the vagina as if he were posting
a letter through a tight slot, looks at the sky as he gropes inside, looks urgently at the sky a little longer (I imagine so

as not to distract his sense of touch), and pulls his hand out suddenly when he confirms Navor's diagnosis.

"Put your hand in," he instructs me, "just straight in." *Quickly*, his eyes say. And without time to worry about the delicacy of it, I plunge my hand into the tight, warm cow, feel her flesh fold around me, until my fingertips bump against something solid.

Involuntarily, I exclaim, "What's that?"

"You'll feel two hooves . . . one here . . . one here." He locates the hooves in the air. "And between them a nose and head."

Everything feels the same. In this blindman's buff, my sense of touch falters. A hoof should feel hard, shouldn't it? Soft things slide past my fingertips.

"You'll feel the split in the hooves, the nostrils . . . keep feeling."

I do, until the tactile fog lifts, and my fingers begin to make sense of what they feel: two hooves, soft and split, a head between them, and a funny bulge.

"You'll probably also feel a tongue sticking out, and that's why we've got to get the calf out of there; it's choking." "Choking," he says without a waver, as if he were saying *the bench is made of wood*. Though he moves with no special alarm, neither does he waste any movements. His face looks dark as a thunderhead.

By now, Navor has set up the birthing crank that has a leather rump halter on one end and a winch on the other at the end of a long pole. While I step clear, to give the men plenty of room, Al loops a chain around his fingers and plunges a hand into the cow again. Once the chain's secure (I'm afraid to ask where), Navor begins the cranking, "pulling" the calf, feet first, out of the heifer, while Al pulls by hand. The feet appear, with a chain bracelet around each fetlock, and the heifer tries yet again to give birth, this time moaning like one of the bombed of Dresden. Suddenly, the knob of an oversized head appears; Al pulls it past the walls of the vagina, and, after that, it's slick sailing—out come a streamlined body and back feet, all encased in a luminous peacock-blue sac, striped with glistening red veins, yellow urine, and patches of iridescent silver. A sea creature has appeared from the heart of a giant abalone. Al rubs a gunny-sack over its head, gently pulling placenta from its mouth and nose, while its huge tongue wags on the ground. No part of it seems alive but the tiniest heartbeat fluttering on its flank as if a moth were trapped under the hide.

"There's a heartbeat!" Al calls, and folds one of its legs to give it artificial respiration. Navor works furiously to clear the mouth and nose, while Al stretches the long spindly leg to full length, then folds it back and pushes gently, as he would with a drowning victim. Nothing. A heartbeat, but no breath. Placental fluids have gotten deep into the lungs, and getting them out will be a hard job. Transfixed, I sit by the fence, watching as the emergency unfolds. Taking the back hooves in their hands, they hoist the calf high in the air, and, to my amazement, begin swinging it massively between them. Back and forth they sweep the heavy calf, still covered in placenta, its grotesque tongue hanging out, its eyes open and motionless. Back to the ground. They check the mouth again, look for breath, give more artificial respiration, and again they lift it between them, groaning from the weight. As a last resort, they toss the calf high over their heads and onto the fence rail, its lungs on one side, its torso on the other, hoping to press the liquid free. Al holds its head tenderly as it hangs over the wooden fence in the sunlight, a poor creature barely present in the world, little more than a heartbeat and a hide.

Like the heifer, I too am stunned by what's passing before me, and am praying the mousy little newborn will drink air. In Al's eyes, I can see possibility flickering, disappearing, flickering, and finally going out. For half an hour, they repeat each step, until the end has indisputably been reached. Dragging the calf off the fence, they try one last time for a heart-beat and breath. Nothing.

"Damn," someone says, exhausted, his voice mapping the full register of defeat. The calf lies in the dirt, motionless as a well-used rag; like Al's jeans, it's coated with blood and afterbirth. Navor leans a thick shoulder against the fence, looking pointlessly at the calf, as we all do. No one wants to give up, but it is over.

"Well, I guess that's all we can do," Al says, peeling off one glove and putting on a fresh one.

"I guess so," Navor says, and drags the limp calf across the corral.

From a box, Al pulls a syringe and some medicine, care-fully gives the heifer a shot in each rump, and takes four large lilac tablets in his hand. Again, he reaches inside of her, but this time well up to his shoulder, reaching deep into the storm-tossed womb where trouble may lie. The lilac pills will help the afterbirth come out, as it must to prevent an infection. Slowly, he removes his long, blood-covered arm, and gives Navor the go-ahead to untie her horns.

Though her calf is dead, she will have other calves other years. Fluky, this trouble may never recur, but it's crucial she learn *how* to mother, so, outside the corral, we watch for a few minutes, hoping that she'll go over to the dead calf and clean it, that her maternal instincts will still be strong. She keeps her distance. Navor shakes his head, in a just-can't-win sort of way, and spits a bit of tobacco. One last possibility remains. Jumping into the pickup, we hurry over to a barn nearby, where there's an orphan calf.

"Normally, we'd skin the dead calf . . . ," Al explains.

"*Skin* the calf?" I'm beginning to wonder what the morning still has in store for me. Death before 8:00 A.M. is about all I can take; skinning I don't think I'm up to. But I mean to learn, as Al knows, and if *they* skin the calf, *I* skin the calf.

"Will we have to do that?" I ask, working hard to keep my

voice even. How could I pull the outer calf from the inner, the fluffy, personalizable baby from the hunk of meat?

"No, I hope not. Where we're headed, you'll see a calf with another calf's hide tied over it. The heifer's natural calf died, and we put an orphan calf on her to suck. The natural calf's skin is so the heifer would think it was her own." He bounces gently through a ditch.

"And that works?"

"You bet it does. That heifer smells her calf, and everybody's happy."

Spare boxes of medicine, a roll of toilet paper, and a pair of gloves jiggle across the dashboard as we follow the bumpy road to a small, open barn. In one stall, an alert, protective mother stands in front of an eerie sight: a calf with a loose, second skin tied around it. As the calf nurses, the mother nuzzles it gently, turning around to shield it even from our view, oblivious to her calf's double coat.

"Smell, it's a wonderful thing," I muse.

"Yep." Al catches the orphan calf, and loads it, an armful of scramble, into the truck. But it's how much smell meant to the evolution of our species I'm really thinking of, the primordial fish leading slender, inert lives who, thanks to the chancy development of a nose, no longer had to sit tight and wait for food to drift by, but could venture out and track it, following the molecular trail of bread crumbs farther and deeper into the water. What with smell warning of danger and trumpeting sex, too, the olfactory tissue must have become swiftly indispensable, growing larger and more complex, until finally it developed into a brain. Whether this myth is any different from other creation myths, I don't know; but it's a fine and private thought to have in the middle of the New Mexico prairie, while a heifer, the wool of smell pulled over her eyes, gives suck to a hungry orphan. I often forget that for most animals smell hits like a sirocco, scouring their senses, and leading them to clear, useful conclusions. Think of snakes, pigs, dogs, rabbits, deer, and others, all sniffing low to the ground where heavy, smell molecules abound; I wonder how it was we came to differ. Somewhere in the long passage from sea to land, and land to trees, we must have swapped our smell for senses more useful to treetop life—seeing and hearing. By the time we really took to the ground, we were upright, and I guess smell mattered less then. Less than taste, for instance, since what entered the body had to be venomless and nutritious, pass the "test" from which our word "taste" derives.

Al interrupts my reverie with an "Okay, we're set," summoning me to the truck for the return drive.

Heartbreaking though the sight is, we pull up to the corral as quietly as possible, and survey the grim relationship between mother and dead calf. Instead of cleaning it, as most mothers would, she stands in wide-eyed horror at the far corner of the enclosure, silent, watchful, numb.

"A bad sign," Al says, shaking his head. "By now I was hoping she'd check the calf out, have it cleaned, be trying to mother."

He tiptoes around the back of the truck, and, with Navor's help, smoothly unloads the orphan, carrying it in his arms to the corral gate, where he sets it inside. What a sight. A dead calf, an orphan calf, and a traumatized mother. Within seconds, the orphan trots over to the heifer and begins a circling nuzzle of her stomach, looking for the soft, rubbery spigots. We try not to move. Miffed, the heifer puts her head down and gives the calf a hefty butt with her horns.

"Oh!" escapes from my lips before I mean it to.

"Give 'em a chance," Al says softly.

The hungry calf nuzzles back at another angle, keeps searching, but there's no mistaking it—he isn't her calf, and so the heifer turns nervously, now and then soundly shoving him away. But she could injure him if she wanted to, indeed, kill a man with one plough of her horns, so, at the moment, it's a battle of nerves, and the calf, diving into her fur with such pluck, refusing to take shove, glower, or butt as an answer, is beginning to just plain wear her out.

"Persistent little rascal, isn't he?" I say.

Al laughs, and it's the first time all day I've seen his face relax. Another butt tosses the calf off balance, but it picks itself up and plunges in again to nurse, this time grabbing an udder and hanging on. What will the mother do, I wonder. She must be painfully full of milk, and the orphan is cheeky enough to have won our esteem, if not hers. She turns her head around and sees, as we do, his tail twitching and flopping (as it usually does when a calf is nursing), and though her regard is still cautious, her senses confused (what's happening *feels* right, but doesn't *smell* right), she is no longer belligerent. I resume chewing the wad of gum in my mouth that has been sitting there, unchewed, for the last hour.

When Al drops me off at the West Bar-T, it's just in time to find Juan and Steve bringing in a ready-to-calve heifer. She also has been having trouble, and the calf will have to be pulled. I don't think I can cope with another death so soon, but the cowboys act so calm, driving the waddling heifer into a stall, tying their horses by draping the reins twice over a fence rail, patiently unpacking the gloves and medicines they'll need, all the while exchanging light banter and talking with me about the weather, the cows, New York State, that I begin to calm down with them, and am ready to help the calf be born, if born it's going to be. I don't imagine you can be a cowboy if you don't believe in fate, the weather, the timing, the Russian roulette of the cells, or, by extension, that your number will be up when it is. For these newborns, fate is often enough a cowboy being at the right place at the right time, and knowing when to drive a heifer to cover to save her calf.

Again I check the calf's position, along with Juan who, for so young a man, is a fine, experienced calver. Everything is in the right place, thank God, for the calf to dive into the world, head between its arms. Never again will I plunge into a swimming pool without remembering how these babies enter the world: diving, hooves first, a placental blindfold covering their eyes. Both men strip off their coats and vests, though it's cold out, and put on surgical gloves up to each shoulder; then Steve fixes the pulling harness around the heifer's rump and gives Juan the chains. A few moments' fumbling inside (Juan, too, I notice, looks away, giving his touch a clearer picture), finds the right spot, just above the fetlocks, and brings his small, sheathed hand back out. Steve starts to crank, and two satanic hooves appear, followed by the tip of a nose, bridge, and, through the cow's eager groaning, a swollen skull. No wonder she had trouble; the calf must be gigantic. Juan pulls with all his might, and with a sucking pop the calf dives full length, in a slipstream of placental fluids.

"Wow," I exhale.

"Pretty neat, isn't it?" Steve says, as he quickly removes the harness, and helps Juan brush the placenta away from the calf's eyes, nose, and mouth. The rest of the cleaning is left for the mother to do. Chains come off each tiny front foot, and the men pick up the back legs, as Al and Navor had done earlier, and swing the calf gingerly between them.

"It's like slapping a baby," Steve puffs, as they sweep the pendulous life back and forth. Muscles in their chests and arms strain visibly through their shirts. Gently, they lay the calf down, and it's clear at a glance how this calf differs from the ill-fated one midwifed earlier. It lifts its head up a little, its dark-blue eyes open and close, its chest roughly swells. Juan takes a front leg, and stretches it to full length, then presses it back against the chest in an even rhythm. Again he cleans out the mouth and nose. A cold day; the calf shivers.

Imagine coming from the snug warmth of a womb to an overcast blustery New Mexico.

"Will he be all right?" I ask Juan, after he medicates the mother, and turns her loose to tend to her newborn.

"I don't know, maybe. We'll see later," he says, and explains that there are many unknowns: whether the calf will be strong enough to stand and nurse, whether the mother will be attentive, whether the calf encountered difficulties in the womb that aren't visible yet. Anyway, it won't be up on its feet for hours, so their best bet is to check the rest of the herd, as they must do twice a day, every day during calving season.

18

Crackerjack is lovely: quiet, and yet surprisingly full of punch. Loping, he seems glad of the exercise; when he jogs, he does it so slowly I lay my reins over the saddle horn and see how far he will jog all by himself.

"I think I've got me a preacher's horse," I tell the others one day, and open my palms like a book. "I could sit here all afternoon reading *Revelations* or something," and as soon as I say it, I imagine what a lark it would be: the fire and brimstone of *Revelations*, in whose mystical extravaganza so many book titles are embedded, while I rode on a horse quiet as a standing pond.

"Yeh, he's a nice quiet horse," Steve says, "and for being that old he's got a lot of energy." Like the Latham girls, Steve ends each phrase with an inflection, which seems to question what he says as soon as he says it. He spits a bit of tobacco into the dirt behind him. Despite his outfit—traditional hat with a small feather tucked into the band, chaps and gloves, down vest and yellow rainslick, and can of chewing tobacco (whose outline you can see through his chaps pocket)—he looks awfully young to be a cowboy. His fair hair and ruddy complexion and, especially, the way his face slides into swift easy smiles, just as Terry's does, always ready for a new thought, a new joke, a new challenge, remind me that despite all his work experience he is still a seventeen-year-old learning about life with relish. His horse, Pride, he keeps under close control, at a tight jog, because it's a runaway (already, the neck shows a nervous lather). An apprentice cowboy doesn't get the choicest horses for his remuda.

Throughout the conversation, Juan has been smothering a laugh, and finally he can't control himself.

"She can ride Charlie," he says.

Steve closes his eyes, shakes his head, and laughs out loud.

"When I first came here," he says, again inflecting the phrase as if he were asking a question, "they told me they had a bronc for me to ride, so the first morning, like I was all set for him. And then Wallace says, no, Charlie here is nice and gentle, and that the others were just teasing me. So I saddle him up, and load him, and we all head out to move cows up the mesa, you know where you were herding one time. . . ." He points to a far string of mesas topped with tall, rich grass and clandestine thickets. "And I ask Mettie what I'm supposed to do. He says to go get those cows over there and bring 'em in, and then go get those other cows and bring *them* in. . . ." He stretches a long arm toward the distant event. "Well, I give ole Charlie a touch with my spurs, and damn if he doesn't just snap in two! He stuck his head down between his legs, and I just kept going up in the air and coming back down again."

Juan says nothing, but his whole frame shakes as he stifles a laugh.

"One more time," Steve says, "and I swear, I think I

could've stuck on him, but all I had hold of was the roping reins, and when I lost my stirrups that last time and he broke again, I just went clean off."

I can picture the scene, all the other cowboys watching the impromptu rodeo from far off, and laughing themselves silly.

"Well, that wasn't the end of it. I get back up on ole Charlie, and go after some of the cows down by the fence line, and everything is just fine. Then, all of a sudden, Charlie bucks me straight off again, and runs all the way back to the pasture gate! Had to walk three miles on foot, moving those cows along the fence!"

Juan's eyes are hidden in the shadow cast by his hat, but I can see the rest of his face in motion, his moustache twitching with silent guffaws. But only his ears are tuned to us; his head he turns to check each heifer as we pass.

"So Mettie," Steve continues, lifting his hat slightly and setting it back down on his head, "he comes riding up finally, and takes me on the back of his horse to the gate, where we chase Charlie around a little first to wear him out, and then I crawl back on him." Steve puts the palm of his hand over his eyes, shakes his head, and slices the air to emphasize his disbelief. "He was good for maybe another hundred yards, and then he throws me off again! This time 'cross a ditch, so my back landed on it. Hit my arm, my chin, my hand . . . boy was I hurt. Next day, Juan rode Charlie."

Juan nods, grinning. And by the way Steve shakes his head again, I can see the event is vivid in his bones as well as his memory.

"Whew," I commiserate, "that's some crummy introduction to a horse."

"Wait. There's more." He spits a bit of tobacco juice onto the tobacco-brown earth. "One day, I come back from town in the morning, and I'd asked them to leave a horse in for me, and damned if there isn't Charlie standing in the corral. So I get up on him *real* careful, and back him around in a circle maybe thirty times or so to wear him out and maybe get him in hand, and the whole morning I'm super careful with him, feeling really mean about him, and giving him a hell of a time. . . . It's only when I get back to headquarters I find out it *isn't* Charlie at all, but one of Wallace's horses that looks like him!"

I can't control myself, and laugh to think of Steve backing that poor horse around in thirty circles.

"Yeh, but now Wallace has got himself one dandy backing horse, if he ever needs one."

No one laughs harder than Steve.

At midday, in addition to the plumbers and cowboys, the mailman, Dick, sits down to eat, arriving as usual at 11:30 to lunch with the hands, and then continuing on his rounds. Other people manage to drift in and get fed, too. Feeding strangers is an age-old ranch tradition; I see no one turned away, and remember reading just that about the hospitality of ranches in the Old West. The meat we have for lunch tastes like delicatessen corned beef, and I'm surprised to learn that it's ham. Cut fresh, nearby, it tastes nothing like the canned varieties I'm used to, the ones that come pressed in strange tear-shapes.

"Funny," I confess to Sherrie afterward, "I guess I always thought of hams growing in the shape of those cans."

Peas, potato salad, macaroni and cheese, chili sauce, beans, and rolls sit on the table along with the large platters of ham chunks. Coffee and Hawaiian cake for dessert (white cake with pineapple and coconut topping, the recipe for which Adelina got from an issue of *Redbook*).

As dishes pass, the world and his wife rib Steve about everything from his eating habits to his rodeo ride on Charlie, but Steve rolls with the punches and dishes them back, even telling Al that he gave me the full story about Charlie.

"You should never be ashamed of being thrown off a horse,"

Al says, and tells how *he* was once thrown off on the same day his dad was returning to the ranch. He had had to meet him at the airstrip, covered in bruises as if he'd been brawling from the moment his dad had left, and somehow work out a plausible explanation.

As each man finishes lunch, he wipes his mouth hard with a napkin, stacks his dishes on top of each other, sweeps any crumbs off the table, thanks Adelina, and puts his dishes in the dishwasher, catching up his hat and gear from the foyer. In less than a minute, he is out the door, and on his way to the bunkhouse or a quiet place to rest for the slim hour that stands between morning work and afternoon work, an hour slim as a cowhand. Dry weather: no boots stand by the bunkhouse door.

After lunch, Al scouts the pastures by helicopter, looking for the cows that have chosen high ground to calve in, and, even from the air, the terrain looks rough. It would cost a cowboy endless hours to check each fold and rockface. In the distance below, Navor drives his rig, spraying dust behind him. Whistling, Al sweeps the helicopter close to the ochre, ribboned mesas for the sheer beauty of it, following one red stripe along the cliff-face until it pales into a sandy escarpment. Then he tilts the helicopter, rolling it in a bowl of air, as we shoot down to glide low over the scrub, rock, and grasses, looking for telltale squares of red hide tipped by white faces. He points, hovering until I see what he does: a heifer and calf blending into the ground cover. On the two-way, badly garbled by vibration, as if his voice were a warbling reed used to vouchsafe instructions to the underworld, he tells Navor where to scout for the animals, by "the red bluff," and back a ways, adding that the "calf looks healthy."

From my window, the red bluff, know as Spivy Mesa, looks wonderfully Egyptian, like pharaoh temples carved along the

Nile, though perhaps it's Al's vibrating voice that reminds me of Karnak temples alive with images of the river: papyrus, rushes, birds, and scarabs rolling the sun toward a new day. Gunning low over the vegetation, we startle two deer, who leap into flight between slatey crags. Antelope on the valley floor, deer in the mountains; evolution prospers by keeping them apart. The deer disappear into a pocket of hillside, *poof!*, like two red handkerchiefs but I prefer how the prong-horn antelope move, in long straight lines, their tail-flags stiff. The mesa deer are climbers, but the valley antelope can run at speeds of 25 m.p.h. over long distances without tiring, and, unlike most galloping animals, they waste little energy in bounding and swerving. Instead, they run straight ahead, their leg muscles heaviest close to the bone so their long, trim legs will be free for fast movement. A large trachea speeds air to the lungs, but, because they would need colossal nostrils for such a trachea, they run with their mouths open to breathe. When frightened, as they were when Al and I buzzed some in the helicopter last June, they tend to run straight. Coyotes, wolves, and other relay hunters, which count on wearing out their prey, would have a hard time keeping up with an ante-lope, its legs whirling as it heads for the horizon. With grass so sparse this time of year, and cattle grazing, one wonders how the antelope could survive; but it's not grass they feed on but less desirable prairie forage: snakeweed, larkspur, fringed sagebrush, bindweed, yarrow, locoweed, and even the needles of the prickly pear cacti (not the blood-red, pomegranate-like fruit).

A swoop into the valley reveals a large, earthen dam, a chunk of which has been washed out by recent floods. How much work must have gone into piling high all that earth is still visible. Al says that one day soon they'll get round to repairing it. He's never mentioned land management to me before, and I'm surprised to learn, over the gyrating roar of the helicopter, how pliable land can be, if you've a mind to re-form it. A detour over one end of the valley shows me a bouquet of small, dammed-up pools.

"Waterholes?" I wonder why the windmills wouldn't be sufficient, and easier.

"Not just that. We're actually filling in the land, damming up there, and over there, so after the water runs at flood it'll leave silt behind."

Surely he doesn't intend to fill in that maze of creekbeds and gashes with just silt.

"You do think in big terms."

"Have to," he says between engine surges; and I can see what a challenge terra-forming could be. There's been some speculation about terra-forming whole planets, such as Venus or Mars, but what I like especially is Al's all-things-are-possible spirit, his frontier confidence that a little elbow grease can solve any problem, and nothing is too big to tackle. Land isn't flat enough? Why, you just fill it in.

"Is all the land I can see yours?" It's an indelicate question, like asking a man how many head of stock he has, which is tantamount to asking him his bank balance, but I hope he'll understand the surprise I feel looking so far down the valley to where the land shrinks to a single line, and the line pales to ether.

"Everything under the rim," he replies, meaning the rim of the mesas, "and some of it beyond."

The ranch is the size of a small principality, and I can see that it would take an army of mounted cowboys a week to cover the land he can scout in less than an hour from the air.

Remembering my delight at helicopter lessons last trip, he takes us up to a safe height and levels out, then passes me the controls which, trembling, I hold lightly, as I would a bird, then swing right as if I were neck-reining a crystal horse. Before we land, he shows me how to hover the craft, which takes more finesse than one imagines, or I can manage. Like patting your head and rubbing your stomach at the same time. I try to hold my airspace without drifting up/down or back/ forth, though inertia is ready to send me at jarring angles. The blue dragonfly, I call his helicopter, but I'll never undervalue a real dragonfly's gyro again.

The afternoon, if not young, is still usable, so Al sends me back to the West Bar-T, where Tom, Terry, Juan, and Steve work together, sorting the cows that have mothered-up well from those that need to be left a little longer. We pass many newborns nursing as they should, their fluffy white faces tucked into their mothers' bellies, and their wobbly legs trying to make sense of the ground. Others can walk now, but bafflement grips them: where are they, *what* are they? How can this unnameable stumbling their legs do carry them from one place to another? Frolicking, they twitch their rumps up higher than their heads, Charleston a few steps, ripple their springy spines; but, when the herd moves, all is confusion. They have not been on the planet long enough to know what *forward* is. Often they stand looking in the wrong direction, puzzled, waiting for fortune to move them. A mother may return and low to her calf, urging it along, but just as often the calf will hold its ground, bleating pathetically.

Bundled up against the weather, in a heavy jacket and a woolen hunter's cap, Tom trots after a confused calf, trying to haze it along. He rides straight at it, flailing his arms and yelling and throwing in a few whistles for good measure, but the calf doesn't budge; understands neither the sounds nor the movements, stands pillar-still, watching the windmilling form approach. Just when it looks as if Tom is bound to run it over, he pulls his nervous horse up short, laughing as he dismounts. Picking the calf up in his arms, he carries it bodily twenty yards or so to where its mother waits. As if that's what it wanted all along, the calf scampers after its mother and toward the rest of the herd, now and then thrusting its nose into her belly, trying to nurse, its tiny heels flicking to one side and the other as it skips, breaks step and trots, runs a little more, stops dead, and skips again, all to keep up with the cow's casual walk.

Heifers and calves we move from one pasture to another, giving them just enough time to mother-up, before shooing them along. Those not mothering well, we leave behind, along with heifers whose calves haven't been cleaned yet. At an arroyo, the cows trot down the slope and leap across, but the calves all bunch on the edge, confused by unfamiliar terrain. After a few minutes' hazing does nothing but mix them into a tighter pool of agitation, the cowboys dismount, hand me all their reins in a heap, and toss the calves into the gulley, one after another, like armloads of laundry, then push them, one by one, up the other side.

While the others mount up, Terry takes the chance to practice a trick mount. Grabbing the saddle horn, he tries to throw himself into the saddle.

"Hey, Roy Rogers!" Tom yells, as Terry's leg, which just misses clearing the back, hits the horse's rump and slides down.

"You're going to leave footprints all over that horse," I say, but, knowing Terry, he'll have the trick mastered by summer.

Daydreaming as we work a heifer back to the barn, I lose track of what's doing and drift in front of her and her calf.

"Whoa!" Tom yells, motioning me back.

"Offside!" I cry, and pivot Crackerjack on one of those rumored "dimes" cutting horses are supposed to pivot on, then keep him in a holding pattern just in back of the cow and calf until the other riders catch up. What they had been hanging back to cabal about I knew I'd learn in good time, and the time seems to be at hand.

"You want to doctor the cow?" Terry asks, taking care not to emphasize the word "doctor." I marvel a human being can pronounce six words with exactly the same stress.

"Oh, sure. After all, I *am* a doctor."

Terry's grin, that I've come to know so well, and dread with such exquisite delight, hits his face like a bucketful of quinine water.

"Are you really a doctor?" Steve asks, taken aback. When his accent makes each of his phrases sound like a question, it's doubly strange to hear him actually pose one.

"Not like a surgeon. I mean I can't pull teeth or set bones. My dear fellow, I am merely a physician of the soul." Slight bow.

The men laugh nervously. I am leading them to the edge of unfamiliar territory.

"Like a doctor of history . . . ?" Steve asks.

"Right. Only *English* in my case."

"Ah," he says, and nods that his question has been answered, if not explained. For a moment, they look at me as if they are peering into the shadowy hollows of a dry well.

Trotting close behind the heifer, I can see part of the stringy afterbirth, like a long ice-cream cone drip, hanging out. Tom explains that we're taking her in to medicate her, since the afterbirth didn't come out by itself, as it's supposed to.

"Down in Deming," Steve says, "when they find a heifer like this, they'd fix her right here. One cowboy'd rope her, and the other'd get two pieces of wood, for holding the afterbirth with, and just pull it out."

"Sounds messy. Also sounds like you'd need a damn good roper."

"Do." His face is alive with the possibility. Juan could rope the horns, working his horse constantly to keep the rope taut, while Steve pulled the afterbirth.

"Down in Deming, you say?" Some of us smile. We all know it's a technique very much taboo on the Tequesquite, since it's much safer to drive the cow to a barn.

Over the rise, between the windmill and the barn, a lone calf lies quietly in the dirt.

"Hey, that calf was here early this morning, too. Where's its mother? Is it sick?" I ask, and learn that it's physically well enough, just neurotic. A week's stay in the stalls, after it was born, made it reluctant to be anywhere else. Now its mother comes by occasionally to feed it; and, ultimately, with any luck, it will wean itself and move along. Around back, between the manure heap and the corral fence, lying with its sorrowful head under the lowest fence rail, is another barn-obsessed calf. Its birth was so chancy that it had to stay under cover for days, and now the barn's dark familiarity is a halfway house from womb to world it can't let go of. By the waterhole, its mother watches and waits. What a fate: to lie in the raw, windy corridor between worlds, catatonic and unreconciled.

"A sorry fellow," I hear myself whispering.

In the barn, the cowboys haze the heifer into a tight-fitting squeeze chute, and ritually present me with a long, flesh-colored glove. Its ample fingers, as I discovered this morning, are obviously meant for men's hands, and it unrolls well over the ridge of my shoulder. Terry hands me four lilac pills the size of field mice, and introduces me to the business end of a breeding cow, while the other cowboys climb the fence above me for a good view.

"Watch the hooves!" Terry cautions, and pulls the swishing tail aside, holding it tightly against the fence. Steve perches high above me, his legs stretched across the fence rails and over my head. It's a strange view wherever I look: in front of me the several back passages of a cow; above me, a cow-boy's long chaps-clad legs, his face peering between them; and either side, twinkling eyes watching between the fence slats.

The cow looses wind, and the cowboys laugh. The longer I take the more nervous she'll get, so I sigh dramatically, and dunk my hand into her, plunging it through a curtain of pink flesh. Her hot, tight walls grab my hand and arm, fold snugly around them, and urge them in deeper. No one is going to make a joke about bulls, but it's in everyone's grin.

"Okay, sport," I look to Terry, "give me some road signs."

He sobers up: "Well, do you feel two round things in there?"

"Like two meatballs," Juan adds helpfully.

My arm full-length inside a cow, my nose uncomfortably close to her rectum, and they're telling me to feel around for two meatballs.

I give Terry a give-me-a-break look. "Are we talking ovaries here, or what?"

Nobody knows. Instead, they give me directions to work my way over the pelvic rise and into a gulley beyond which are two meatballs and then a sharp ridge that plunges into the womb.

"Are we talking about ovaries," I repeat, "kidneys, wombs, rises, windmills, what the hell are we talking about?"

As earlier, when I'd felt a calf in the vestibule of a vagina, I struggle to release my sense of touch, give it full rein, and tune my other senses down, if possible let my need to interpret wash away. Long minutes I grope aimlessly in the hot wallow. What the cow makes of all this I can't imagine.

Steve tucks a plug of tobacco into his lip. Juan wonders if it's getting to be dinnertime.

"This is all very embarrassing," I lament, "I mean, you'd think a woman would know another woman's anatomy. I'd be less lost in Calcutta."

Trying to fathom the mink-soft recesses, my mind primes one image after another: sand dunes, piles of coal dust, chinchilla pelts, moss-lined arroyos. If I let my senses shift focus, I know my brain will start inventing things to help the flagging touch make do. My senses are nothing if not loyal. Concentrating, I spread my gloved fingers, and try to imagine them as pristine and perceptive as the *Viking* lander's exploratory arm.

Juan's stomach growls, and he goes to fetch another glove from the storeroom, says nothing, but comes up gently behind me, waiting for me to pull out. It's a compromising position, up to your shoulder inside a cow. Juan looks down at me with dark, sympathetic eyes.

"We'll be here till midnight."

Nodding, I carefully withdraw my effluvium-coated arm, feeling the heifer's muscles ungrip me stage by stage, as if releasing a long line of handshakes. Flexing, she pushes me out the last few inches.

"I'm sorry; it's so damned confusing in there."

"That's okay," Terry says, "but it's getting late. And Juan's getting hungry."

Juan laughs, and reaches his arm deep into the heifer, as if lunging with a rapier, deposits his stash of medicine, and neatly withdraws.

Before dinner, I drag myself back to the trailer to wash. The small of my back hurts miserably, and so does the top of each thigh, just under the gluteals. After the first four or five hours in the saddle, to ease my sore rump when we had to lope a long distance, I'd reach a hand behind me and grab hold of the saddle, pressing myself tighter to it for a few strides. But still I ache in too many places to point to, and, at the same time, feel so sensuously saturated and exhausted, I can't say for sure how many weeks I've just spent in the last twelve hours. Now I know the advantage of having showers in all the buildings, instead of bathtubs: it's harder to fall asleep standing up.

19

One day, after breakfast, we meet in the corral as usual, to rope our horses, say hello, and part ways for work. Al suggests that I do rounds with Mettie today, checking the older cows in the giant pastures. To my surprise, Crackerjack is not there; Mettie has asked them to bring in the quietest of his fiery remuda, a chestnut named Chapeau. He hasn't forgotten that he'd promised to let me ride one of his crazy, beautiful horses, but he's waited until he could be with me, just in case. Lyn whispers that Chapeau is very nervous, trots super fast, and doesn't really jog at all, so be prepared. Her eyes jump with caution.

Once we've loaded our horses, Mettie waits at the trailer doors for me to close them, and I realize what poor attention I've been paying to such details. Five separate movements close the interlocking bolts and flanges. I move a few bolts clumsily, then get it right. He nods.

"*Vamos,*" he says, jumping into the truck. A slap against the closed door summons his dog, who leaps onto the flatbed of the truck and barks furiously. A pair of fine, cream-colored gloves lies on the seat between us, like two matched doves. One fingertip is raggedly torn.

"Pretty gloves."

Mettie spits tobacco into a tiny orange-juice can sitting on the dashboard.

"Cost me twelve dollars just two weeks ago, and now look what happened while I was fixing a windmill." He holds up the tattered finger. The rest of the gloves look butter-smooth and unused; I slip one on and stroke it over my cheek.

"Watch it! You don't know where those have been," he warns with a wink. The netherparts of a cow.

It's a welcome chore to do rounds with Mettie again; what with all the bustle and drama of calving we really haven't had a chance to say more than hello. In each pasture, we drop feed cake for the cows, calling them with the truck's siren, and circling slowly as cake rolls out of a bin. Scattered across the enormous, rolling pastures, often the cows are too remote to hear the sound of the siren, and we round them up on horseback, riding away from the truck until it disappears into a fold of country, locating the cows, and then herding them back the way we came, each time covering a tremendous rush of land. I pull my fluffy hat down low against the cold winds. Mettie, too, pulls his hat down lower, so the brim will keep the wind and glare from his eyes, tucks his chin into his thermal coat, under which is a thermal vest and a heavy shirt. Each time he spots a stray cow, he tells me so, but not where it is, and waits patiently for my eyes to focus on each sector of scrub prairie and mesa line, finally pointing it out over and over as we move closer to it. But the more I strain my eyes against the kaleidoscopic horizon, the more tonal everything becomes. Now and then, I get lucky, and on something that looks like sagebrush in the distance, a white dot floats—the white face of a Hereford. Another white dot by its shoulder tells me there is a calf. Mettie points out a herd of "black bears" along a mesa.

"Bears? A herd of grazing bears?"

He laughs and says no more. If I'm too naive to figure out they're Black Angus steers, it's my look-out.

The constant winds can fade into the wallpaper of one's waking life so completely. At first they were everywhere, blustery and distant, like gas burning off the jets of an oil rig, and now I notice them only when we trot and air rushes by so quickly it sounds as if we're scything a field of wheat.

"What are those rifles and that handgun for?" I ask as we jog a cow back to the feed. "Expecting bandits?"

"Prairie dogs, coyotes, that's all."

A coyote is just large enough to attack a newborn calf, and a gang of coyotes could hold its own on a lively patch of veldt. I remember Al's telling me how one day he and Steve went coyote hunting from the helicopter. Before long, Steve shot a coyote on the run, and they zoomed down to load the carcass aboard before taking to the skies for another salvo. The next coyote, Steve shot in the shoulder; it dived into a hole, so Al set the copter down nearby, and Steve jumped out to try to pull the coyote out by its tail, but its back legs locked firmly against the walls of the burrow. When two rifle shots in the rump still didn't kill it, Al got his shotgun out and finished it off, dragging what was left of the carcass to the helicopter, and tossing it in the back with the other. To their alarm, they heard a vicious bark. The first coyote was still alive, and in a foul humor about having a dead relation tossed on top of him.

Mettie strokes Nitro's neck, where a thick, sudsy lather has welled up. A nervous horse, Nitro tosses his head obsessively, prances, and sweats. But on his saffron hide even the sweat looks pretty, a bit of white water on the rippling sands of his muscles. Neither horse will walk quietly, but both lope in gentle cradle gaits as slowly as other horses jog. It's the gait that characterizes all of Mettie's horses, and without it, riding them would be a constant battle. Against a far fence stands a handful of cows. I count six, but Mettie says there are eight, and I know enough to trust both his hunch and his vision. Chapeau launches into a whirlaway trot so fast I can hear fists of yucca being stirred by the breeze of his legs. Sitting deeper into the saddle, I try to relax, and fix my hands unyieldingly at the saddle horn until he relaxes too, and settles into a slower pace. Mettie has broken five horses since I last saw him, and it's strange to think of a man so volatile breaking horses with the patience of Job.

"It's true," he says, "lose your temper with one, and you might as well forget working it that day, because it won't be any good."

The curly black hairs of his beard drag back in the wind. Under the black felt brim of his hat, his dark eyes look even darker, and on his hands the pale creamy flesh of his new gloves reminds me of those sides of him one rarely sees.

At each station, he counts the cows and jots down the figure in ballpoint pen on the knee of his chaps. So many cows and calves come for feed at one stop they circle around the truck like an Indian war party.

"Count them," Mettie directs me, after he has counted them twice. But where do you begin when everything is in flux? I try a structure: pretend the red herd is an orange, cut it into segments, count the white-faced pips in each segment.

"Seventy-two, seventy-three, seventy-four . . . ," I say, coming full circle.

"Eighty-two," Mettie says matter of factly, "try again."

This time I picture a world map whose latitude lines start at the truck and bulge to the horizon. A paradox springs suddenly to mind: *God is a circle whose center is everywhere and periphery is nowhere*. I point one finger, as I'd seen Mettie do,

ticking it at each cow, and dipping it sharply at each calf, as
if it were divining water.

"Seventy-seven, seventy-eight . . . rats!"

A final time. I think of the truck as a sun, from which
orange-red rays of light pour in clear straight beacons, between which there is nothing but blank space. All that is color
must fall into one of the beacons; and as colors drift from one
beacon to the next, I try to sort them.

"Eighty."

Close enough. We get back into the truck. Mettie flips on
the radio like downing a drug, and Charlie Pride warbles into
Crystal Gayle into Debbie Boone. Between songs, we chat
about the news, the songs, the ranch, the tempo of our lives.

"Your English is gangbusters all of a sudden, *amigo*."

He looks pleased. "I've been learning it at night, at school."

"Uh huh, that's what I hear. Give you a kind of specialized
vocabulary though, no?"

He looks sideways, downshifts the trailer to run up the hill,
and shifts back into drive when we clear the rise.

"What have you heard?"

"Oh, nothing . . . I'm just guessing in the dark."

"What have you heard?"

"Not a damn thing, not a damn thing."

He stops the truck, looks me straight in the eyes, with
the same don't-fool-with-me-if-you-know-what's-good-for-you
stare I saw in the eyes of his dog when I'd startled it at sunrise. When I smile, his bluff evaporates. He knows I know.
And he knows I know he doesn't care. Mettie has fallen for
the new schoolmarm, whom he's been seeing hot and heavy
ever since she arrived. And it's just the sort of romance to
keep the ranch gossip in clover. Becky, the lily-complexioned
eastern schoolmarm, and Mettie, the swarthy roustabout.
Schoolmarming used not to be so comfortable, and it's no
wonder the New England women who went in for it, risking

poor supplies, rotten buildings, bad lodging, and obstreperous students, would often do so only out of evangelical or matrimonial motives. In many places, they had no steady home, but were obliged to bunk with the family of each student in turn, usually living in a one-room cabin, a corner of which had been partitioned by a sheet. Two dollars a week was average pay, and textbooks frequently were nothing more daring than almanacs, proverb sheets, and Bibles. A tough life it was, made even tougher by such frontier problems as Indians, boredom, and the plague.

Becky's only student, for the time being, is Lyn Mitchell, and her classroom is a gem of updated Americana. I hear Becky is a secure, self-possessed young woman, a bit of a loner, who keeps to herself and her trailer most evenings. What will happen when Lyn goes away to high school in two years, and a schoolmarm is no longer needed, is anyone's guess. Mettie doesn't risk an answer.

"I gave up all my bad habits," he says flourishing a hand.

I lift my eyebrows so high he reconsiders.

"I gave up *most* of my bad habits . . . don't fight anymore, don't smoke—chew, but don't smoke—don't drink . . . women I won't give up . . . but the others—I'm getting too old for it. I stay on the ranch now nights so I don't get into trouble." He means in the bars of Logan, a good place for pandemonium.

Mettie and I are the same age, and it's been a watershed year for me, as well. Still, only a few months ago, before he met Becky, he was young enough to blister the county.

"That song," he says, turning up the radio, "it's about you. Listen."

Through a haze of country guitar twang, I hear a man singing about a lady writer who seems to live an exciting life, but isn't really content with it.

"It's about you, no?"

My heart begins to pound, and it takes me a few moments

to collect myself. The change in my relationship with Mettie is extraordinary. He has read what I've written about him, and knows he can trust me, trust what I will *not* say, for instance. And there is a new, complex edge to his protectiveness; that he will not let me fall into danger, I feel as absolutely as I know the sun is in the sky. I would transfer my life to his protection at a moment's notice. But short of crisis, he seems eager for me to be on my own, make my own mistakes. My motives seem newly clear to him. When others are around, face matters, and he razzes or takes little notice of me, but alone together, as we truck from one pasture to another, leaving a trail of feed cake behind, we talk with the easy candor of old friends.

"Funny how you can get so professionalized that you end up doing what you're good at instead of what you enjoy."

He nods. "You mean being a teacher."

"I'm a good teacher now; it would be a waste of life to make a living any other way. And I've really grown to enjoy teaching, it isn't that . . . but I don't think there's anything on the face of this planet more *fun* than working all day on horseback. Out of doors, with animals, stretching your limits, working way past exhaustion. And I have the strangest hunch the novelty wouldn't wear off after a few months. It's so lovely to be outside watching the land change color, the creekbeds fill and empty, the herds grow, the weather parch or steam or gust or hang still. . . . And you, you're too good a cowboy by now to do anything else either, no?"

"Yes, but I like it," he says, "really. Like you say, it's good to work outside, with a horse and the weather changing and the cows. It's always different." He brings the orange-juice can to his lips and lets a drop of tobacco juice fall into it. I can see a question forming on his face.

"When you write about something, do you always need . . . need . . ."

"To fall in love with it?"

"Yes."

"I guess so . . . I don't know why exactly, but I seem to fall in love with ideas the way other women fall in love with men."

He smiles.

I know he's not talking about my poetry writing, and it's about that, the real panic and privilege of my life, that I ought to be answering him. But how can I tell him that compared to the sensuous red-alert of the adventurer-me he knows, the one ready to trek off to the South Pole, or ocean bottom, at a moment's notice, the poet-me is a hundred times more intense, sponging up the flavors and sights of every minute, as if it will be my last, moved to tears by scanty flashes of bright red on the delicate plumage of a female cardinal, easily wowed by a surge of wind visible only in the twirling leaves of a silver birch.

After lunch, Mettie gives Steve and me a lift to the West Bar-T, on his way to work the rest of his pastures. Between the men, on the bouncing truck seat, I feel like a tennis net as they lob gentle insults, and every twenty yards or so, apropos of nothing, I ram my left foot onto Mettie's on the gas pedal, hard enough to lay rubber to Denver. Without looking down, Mettie braces his foot at exactly the right instant so that all the truck does is bounce an extra time or two. Steve notices none of this, and merely comments that the road sure is rough. A muffled laugh Mettie disguises with a cough. Neither of us says a word; conversation continues, about calves and the ranch, and, after another twenty yards when I jam Mettie's foot down again, again, he catches mine in time. The faintest smile rises on his face. As if nothing out of the ordinary had happened in ten years, he calmly picks up his orange-juice spittoon and dribbles a bit of tobacco juice into it, while simultaneously bracing his foot against my latest attack. And in this strange, secret, bouncing bolero rhythm we progress, turning at last down the road to the West Bar-T. Mettie begins giving Steve a locker room pep talk about going out with older women, in such flagrant detail, that Steve embarrasses hotly, blushes a hard tomato-red, fidgets with his hat, and starts to sweat. All I can do is twitch with laughter. How to take part, I wonder.

"Listen, Steve," I say in Terry's tone of rehearsed innocence, "Mettie's taught me something to say that would endear me to you. . . ."

"I know *all* those words," he says, wiping the air with one hand, and looking ready to leap from the truck.

"What words?"

"All those that start with *vamos a.* . . ."

At last we get to the barn, and Steve jumps out, hurrying the horses from the trailer. Mettie waits while we check our girths and mount up.

"Now that barn there's a good place," he says, leaning through the window and pretending to appraise it for comfort.

"Mettie!" Steve yells, and pulls his horse around sharply. He is blushing so hard I wonder he has any blood left in the rest of his body.

"Now, you be gentle with him," he instructs me, wagging a finger.

"I'll try, Mettie, but you know we eastern women are like vultures."

"That's what I hear." He slips the truck into drive, and brings it through a half circle, waving as he pulls out.

"See you later, *amigo*," I wave a hand he sees in his rearview mirror, and he replies in kind.

"Boy, that Mettie!" Steve breathes more easily, as we jog toward the creekbed where Juan will already be working.

"Funny exchange over the two-way this morning. Did you hear it?"

He pulls his hat down lower, lest it be pried off by the wind.

"You mean Sherrie and Al going over their grocery list? Yeh, that was funny."

Steve rests his reins-hand on the saddle horn, and lets his eyes follow the dirt as we jog.

"Mettie, he told me I was to let you do everything," he says, and sounds a little surprised that I wouldn't have told him that myself. "I didn't know that."

"Yes, everything. No pampering." But I know it will be quite a while before I have the courage to pull a calf by myself, and be responsible for its life—or death. Courage isn't exactly what I mean, but neutrality.

"Okay. You spot the ones that are ready," he says as we approach a cluster of cows and calves. "See any?"

What, I wonder, would I see? "There's one over there with its tail up all right."

Steve laughs. The cow is just getting ready to relieve herself.

"How about that one?" I point to a low-slung, round-bellied cow.

"You think she's ready, huh? When?"

"Oh, any minute now?" I get set to go after her, in case.

"Gonna take a little longer than that," he drawls, his face a picture of warring jokes. The cow I want to deliver is fat all right, but barren.

"Barren? As in *not bearing*?"

He nods, points under her belly to where the udder bag should be heavy and distended. Sure enough, her bag is barely visible. Nature, for all its faults, wouldn't evolve a cow that calves and give it no way to nurse.

"Ah, I see."

A shadowy figure on the horizon is Juan; even I can tell the charcoal apparition is a mounted horseman. On a mud bridge, we cross from one side of the creekbed to the other, splitting up to encircle a few head of cattle, one of which fidgets and stirs, lying down only to stand up again. Clear signs. Juan approaches at speed.

"That one. And now."

"Right," Steve says, and gentles her along. There's no sense hurrying since, as it is, she can barely walk. Her vagina has begun to stretch, grow loose as a turkey's wattle, and her legs sweep under an enormous, swollen belly as she jogs, one tiny hoof after another, toward the barn. When Juan arrives, we look like three horsemen of the apocalypse jogging straight abreast after the billowy, cleft-footed incarnation of evil, Steve's and my horses in a nervous lather, and Juan, as ever, riding steady as a statuette.

A crease in the earth appears out of nowhere, as often they do on such deceptively flat land. The cow breaks to the right. Without thinking, I twitch my wrist and roll my shoulder, neck-reining Chapeau, to cut the cow off at the right moment. For those slow-motion seconds, I know how it feels when cowpunching works right—the timing, the message to the horse, the shadow-boxing with the cow to steer her without ever making contact.

"Good work, cowgirl," Steve says, and I'm touched. I've helped move, sort, herd, and drive cattle before, but he means that this time the machinery is invisible.

At the barn, I hang back to guard one exit, while the men chase the cow through the corral gate. How strange to control something as large as a cow just by changing where you move in relation to her. So taken am I by the sheer sorcery of it, I'm tempted to lift my hands into a Merlin pose and say "*poof!*"

"Git on," I call instead.

How can the wind still be howling, I wonder. Relentless, it sounds like someone blowing into the thin neck of a pop bottle, blowing cold winds and dust out of the abstract nothingness of a cardinal sign called South. But blow it does. Juan offers me one of his own vests, and I slip into it gratefully, sliding it over my turtleneck sweater, and under my ski jacket and rain slick, until I look plumply quilted as a bed.

* * *

At night, as I lie beneath the "comforter" whose name I feel in the pockets of warmth around my body, I try to fall into a swift, deep sleep so I can rise refreshed for once, instead of starting the day with fatigue, and moving through new fatigues to the final one that carries me back to my bunk at nightfall. But when I close my eyes, I see cattle on a prairie, a clear slide show against my closed eyelids. A spider's web of gray fences leads across a pasture where cowboys are sorting cows by a gate. Bunches of sagebrush, their long leaves coated with dust, are thick but not yet fragrant. I can track across the vision, to where a cowboy, unrecognizable in the high contrast of the eyelid vision, comes to the crumbly edge of an arroyo, leaning back in the saddle, as his horse picks its way down the steep wall, and leaning forward, close to its neck, as he climbs up the other side. Sleep comes only after long stretches of pasture land reel across my vision, when the soughing of the blustery winds gives way to the heavy sounds of my breath.

20

Five-thirty: I swing my legs out of bed, and push the rest of my body up onto them. In a saucepan I make coffee the fastest way: handful of coffee to one cup of water, toss into a pan and boil. Then I lard sunscreen cream all over my face; I wouldn't leave the trailer without it, but I have long since stopped setting my hair or taking special care with make-up. On the other hand, some feminine things are essential, and have been ever since I first started in branding season a year ago. None of the neutral, hard, and dirty work offends my femininity as such; yet I find myself wearing frillier and frillier underthings the dirtier and sweatier I work. No cow notices the splash of cologne in the morning, the clean-shaven legs, the lace, under yards of leather chaps, grimy boots, ripped and restitched jeans, shirts which sweat soaks from the tip of the cuff to the underfold of the collar, and built-up, nearly archeological, layers of dirt. But *I* know, and it helps me keep things in perspective. To be a woman, and do what cowboys do, is not the same as to wish to be a cowboy compleat.

In the blue-blackness, my sense of a sun on the rise just below the horizon is keen, and it's hard to keep science clear in mind. Soon a pale gust of light will drift up from the ground, loosen the starry shingles of darkness, and spit color in wide plumes above the valley floor. After that, the sun rising visibly. A sleepy mind cautions a mind that elsewhere would never dream of questioning a thing like the earth's rotation. But dawn is still to come; my reflection on the black glass tells me it could be nightfall. Again I check the clock, whose loud, rigid ticking drives into my sleepiness like repeated blows on a single nail.

As Wallace and Navor give me a lift to the West Bar-T after breakfast, they tell me about a strange, deformed calf that was born twisted up like a volleyball. It had a curved spine, and all four legs came out together, with the entrails hanging out the other end.

"How on earth did that happen?" I ask Wallace, whose face looks grimy with suntan.

"Maybe its mother was smoking marijuana when she was young," he says dryly. For someone as interested in genetics as Wallace is, such a birth is a fascinating puzzle. He lifts a cannister of chewing tobacco out of his pocket and loosens the lid by twisting it back and forth as if he were pressing a cookie-cutter into dough. "It might have something to do with the locoweed or some wild tansy, say, that the cow might have eaten, just like a pregnant woman could get too much of some drug that might bother her." With three fingers, he pinches a little tobacco. "We'll have to try to figure it out." He fits the tobacco into the right spot under his lip and consults the gray, empty sky. "Thought for sure it would rain yesterday." Moisture is so unusual and so necessary that when people refer to rain or snow they remember the

exact day on which it fell. "We had three and a half inches
back there on November sixth," Wallace says, "and another
five inches on December seventh. In February, it dropped
twelve inches overnight; didn't freeze; was the most useful
precipitation we had."

When I tell Wallace about the heifer we found with twins
yesterday, he explains that twins aren't all that rare, but a
funny thing happens: if you have a male and a female, the
male will be all right, but the female will be sterile, what's
called a "freemartin," because of the effect of the male
hormone on the egg.

Navor starts to fiddle with his long, twirlable moustache,
wrapping one of its waxy ends into a curlicue, and finally asks
Wallace if that's always the case. Wallace laughs, and reassures him that, for some reason, it isn't true of human beings.
Navor, with twins of his own, Gene and Gena, sighs and
relaxes.

At last we pull into the West Bar-T, where Wallace and
Navor leave me with Crackerjack, instructing me to head out
toward the gas plant to find Steve and Juan. The sun is hot
as summer itself, a shapeless, burning, white blister in an
otherwise empty sky: white, not yellow. I hear the rattle of
the horse trailer in the distance, see the dust it kicks up, but,
if I didn't know they had just driven off, I might guess that it
was a bit of wind blowing some light soil around. Under foot,
the ground is packed tight, and cracked for long stretches, as
if the earth had shattered. Clumps of yucca are not yet in
bloom. In winter, the yucca pods split open like milkweed,
and grazing cows spread the seeds by brushing against them.
When the stalks come up, cows take to it the way we do to
asparagus; you can tell they've been eating it by the green
froth around their mouths.

A tumbleweed rolls across the ground like a fur ball, leaving
a tiny wake of dust. It seems motorized, but at the same time
so airy and fragile, following the path of least resistance,

running in the wind down toward the creekbed, scampering like a Mad Hatter with a tea party to get to. Enthralled by the tumbleweed, I don't notice Steve and Juan riding toward me with a plump heifer, until they are only yards away. Tapping Crackerjack with my heels, I perk him up, and jog a wide circle around the men, coming up behind them to join ranks.

"See that cow?" Juan says, pointing far ahead. "See?"

We wait seconds for my eyes to adjust to the strain of spotting detail against the mesas. I am still in the dark, wrinkling my nose and trying to capture the unseen in my focus, when Juan starts to laugh. There is no cow.

"Learn a little English," I sigh, "and you're as bad as your brother-in-law."

Actually, Juan has learned a lot of English, and quickly, with no little help from Susie's new chattiness. It's the first I've seen of Juan's antic side, which goes along with the gentle stock handler, the expert roper and rider, the shy work-man who prefers to ride sections of land by himself, and always used to be eye-of-the-storm silent when I was around. Still quiet for the most part, he breaks his long silence with observations that give me pause. When we pass a calf scratch-ing its ear with one leg, he nods to it and says, "Calf playing the guitar." I've come to respect Juan's concern with the calves; no one seems more attuned to them bodily than he.

One day, we had to milk a full-bagged heifer into a Seven-Up bottle, which Juan showed me how to do by gripping the udders firmly and pulling them at an angle. Then we bottle fed the milk to an ailing calf. Juan had held the listless calf tenderly, putting its head on my knee, and the bottle's nipple in its mouth, lifting the bottle high, urging the calf to suck. When that didn't work, he put a finger in its mouth, between the nipple and the tongue, pressing gently to shoot milk down the calf's throat. A long, tiring process. We spelled each other, until we could be sure the calf would have enough milk to sustain it. The next day the calf was dead. Surely Juan had known it would be, but his tenderness held fast.

In a dry creekbed, off to the right, lies a dead, half-eaten calf, its ribs exposed, and part of its hide still intact. Steve points out the scratches in the dirt that are coyote and crow tracks. First the coyotes pluck the eyes out and eat the tongue, he tells me; on this one, they seem to have gone for the umbilical next. So many years worth of lives and deaths have happened since I arrived for calving season, I don't even flinch at the sight of the carcass open in the sunlight, its ribs like the exposed hull of a boat. Nonetheless, Steve changes the subject.

"You ever heard of monkeys on the prairie?"

Neither Juan nor I have, and it's so clearly the beginning of a yarn, we wouldn't say so if we had.

Steve continues. "Well, down in southern New Mexico, at the Diamond A Ranch, I hear they have spider monkeys running wild. And boars, too. I met this guy who worked there, and he says he roped one of those monkeys once, hoping to drag it to death and find out what it was, when the thing ran up the rope after him and bit him on the shoulder!"

"I don't know, Steve. . . ." I pull my hat down lower and shake my head. "Lassoing monkeys that run up ropes. . . ."

"That's what he says. They like to had a zoo out there, with all sorts of wild animals running around."

Actually, I'd heard similar stories about just such a ranch, but what a vision: acres of cowboys, cactus-strewn prairie, cows, and jungle animals. Like a Latin-American novelist's dream of America.

At the barn, we drive the waddling heifer into one of the stalls, dismount, and leave our horses in the corral to snuffle at bits of straw in the dust. Some patterns are irresistible: each horse a chestnut with its head down, each tail blowing the same in the breeze, the same straps and buckles hanging from each saddle, the three saddle horns rising like the tops of three pyramids. Inside, while the cowboys get ready for birthing, I watch how the sun, coming through the slots in the corral, makes gold lines broken by shadow into ingots of light. Here and there a fleck of straw glitters. Sun cutting through one of the wire gates turns it into a musical staff, on which small opacities appear as eighth notes. Again I marvel that when you stand inside the barn, out of the absolute glare of the sun, the outside world looks like a heat mirage, painfully bright, as if the air had been clarified, boiled off until all that remains is solar vapor. The distant windmill twirls like a sunflower, petaled blades and dark center. A crow riding an updraft planes low around the tank, hovers for a moment, and settles on the rim. The wind has begun to ruffle the manes of the horses, picking up the long hairs, blowing them straight up, and separating them. Even the truck aerial sways regularly in the breeze, and I follow its metronome for a few bars. There's no place you can go on the prairie that you don't hear the white noise of the wind, steady and rough as surf curling along a nonexistent shore. The cowboys open and close metal gates, and the creaks conjure up every prison movie I've ever seen. With a vista as empty as this, everything man-made looms large: the creak of a gate, the complexity of a glove. A single bottle, lying half-shattered by a post, looks exotic as a tiny Crystal Palace.

A pool of blood in one of the stalls shines like paint in the sunlight, and a single fly walks across it, in and out of the shadow cast by the fence slat. A cowboy could walk into the barn, knowing nothing of what happened yesterday, read these signs, and know everything.

Steve and Juan go about their business, rearrange some of the cows and calves in other stalls, and tie the heifer's horns snugly against a fence. Normally, I would help. But when they see that my thoughts are fully employed elsewhere, they leave me to my reverie.

When I first came to the ranch, I couldn't get the cowboys to talk at all. I still shudder when I remember the lunches that passed with no noise but that of cutlery! In shipping season, they began slowly, carefully, to talk with me. When I arrived for calving season, they talked constantly, as if wishing to explain themselves. Now, finally, we've come full circle, and they feel comfortable enough not to *have* to talk.

When the cowboys take off their coats and vests, I know it's time for business. A look from Juan asks simply if I am in this hand or out. The heifer begins to struggle against the rope, which Juan slackens a little. She must have room to lie down if she needs to, but not enough to endanger us, or twist herself up. Like the others, I strip off my coat and lay it neatly on a bundle of hay, then fit a surgical glove over my hand and up to my shoulder. Steve looks at the long shafts of hair hanging from the bottom of my hat, and wonders on which day the unavoidable will happen.

"Placenta shampoo," I insist, "people pay a lot of money for it back East. We could bottle it." Juan shakes his head. People back East must be nuts. When the heifer kicks back smartly with a hoof, Juan reminds me that sideways is a better angle of approach, less of a target for her to hit. I slide a gloved hand into the neck of her swollen vagina to feel for the hot nose and soft hooves of the calf. Inside the womb, a calf's hooves are soft and yellow; after birth they harden and grow white very quickly; but, if for some reason they don't toughen as they should, or become injured, the calf will have to be destroyed. Life means grazing, and grazing means motion.

"I think it's okay," I tell them, but Juan checks too, to make sure.

"You didn't feel the tongue?" he says, looking at me, his one hand groping inside her to recheck.

"I didn't," I say. He does.

Juan pulls his hand out quickly and gives me the chains to lace around the calf's fetlocks. One chain I loop like a bracelet around my fingers, holding it in place with my thumb, then ease my hand back into the cow, and try to slide the chain off my hand and onto the calf's foot. Precious seconds I spend fumbling with one hand, then two, trying to locate the right spot, and slide the chains onto it. Juan helps, and soon the chains are in place, bulky ankle bracelets that will drag the calf into March. Steve starts the winch pulling, while Juan and I fold back the walls of the vagina, as if we were turning her inside out. Two hooves appear, shackled clumsily, and then a nose; as the head pushes out, Juan wipes the face at once, and suddenly I can see why: a large, swollen tongue hanging out of the mouth shows the calf is choking. When the heifer falls to the ground, we hold the half-born calf out of her way, readjust the winch, and continue pulling, until the gorgeous peacock-blue sac rushes out, glistening, throbbing, covered with veins of red, saffron-yellow, and silvery-green. Steve unchains its feet, and I run for a gunnysack to start wiping the placenta from its nose and eyes, taking care to wipe well within its mouth. So far, it seems alive, but its tongue is swollen too large for the mouth. Juan and I lift the calf up between us, and begin swinging it back and forth. I know that at all costs I mustn't let it drop, or its tongue will drag in the dirt and make breathing impossible, but it weighs so much all my shoulder muscles yank hard from the bone. I can feel my arms pulling gently out of their sockets, and I must bend my knees a little just to brace myself against the weight.

"Heavy?" Juan looks at me with concern, perhaps judging whether or not Steve will have to take over for me.

"Yes, but it's okay. I can do it," I gasp, and continue swinging the long length of calf, nearly falling, as we carry it into a free area of stall, and lay it down. With the gunnysack, I wipe its face again. The calf's chest swells lightly, but not regularly, so, pulling a front leg out, as I've seen Al and Juan do, I press it gently back against the chest, then pull it out again to full length, and press again, in a light, steady rhythm. The calf lifts up its fluffy head and looks at me, its dark-blue eyes trying to focus, its tongue roaming. I fold the tongue back into its mouth, only to see it flop out again.

"Welcome to the world, little calf," I say, as I wipe the dirt from its tongue, and rub away the last of the beautiful blue chrysalis in which it has lived for nine months. Now the sky will be its blue home; it's only come from one birth to another. Small, yellow hooves are still soft and too tender from the chains to let it stand.

"Welcome to the world, little butterfly," I say, stroking its curly white head. And in its eyes is the absolute bewilderment of the newly born; I've never seen anything so shocked just to be alive. A moment ago, the even black nowhere of the womb, and now all this color and commotion. It trembles with amazement, looks shell-shocked. Am I its mother? What is a mother? What is an I? With my white face and storm cloud of black hair perhaps I am a relation. My palms lick his fur. I make soft noises as I stroke his big ears and fluffy face, soothing, welcoming the ultimate immigrant. As new as this, his face looks mashed in and dwarf-size, his hair clotted with womb saps and dirt, his ears big enough for a grown bull. The bushy shank of white fur between his eyes and over his forehead is just starting to dry in the air.

Thrill rushes through me. How could I see so many calves born and never feel it? This life is mine, and I feel so close to it, so bound to the flutter of its tiny lashes and the fragile puff of its chest. I want to name it.

"*Mariposa*," I say to Juan, and then translate for Steve. "Butterfly."

"Mariposa?" Juan repeats, and makes a butterfly with his hand. Why would I want to call a bull "Butterfly"?

"Well, I hope he doesn't live up to his name."

Juan laughs.

"But holding him like this, and feeling him tremble from the cold, or from just being here at all . . . I don't know, *Mariposa* just seems right."

The startled eyes still study me. How long, I wonder, will the amazement last? For hours, Mariposa won't be able to stand, so we must untie the mother's horns, and let her tend to him, while we ride out to look for other heifers in trouble. But I'm much too enraptured by the tiny life I've just mid-wifed to want to leave. Steve and Juan persuade me to finish rounds with them anyway; and I can see in the way they smile, watching me, that they find on my face the same amazement I find on the face of Mariposa.

"So, that's what it's like . . . ," I say as we saddle up, trying to catch a glimpse of Mariposa through the fence.

Steve holds his reins on the saddle horn, lifts his left foot into the stirrup, and swings the other one up. "Makes a difference, doesn't it?"

It does.

Only the next morning is Mariposa up and sucking, but the udders are too stiff and gorged with milk to make nursing easy for a calf whose tongue is still so swollen. He keeps licking them and trying to get them into his mouth, and we laugh when an udder goes into one side of his mouth and out the other. Now the heifer is all alertness, turning to keep herself between us and Mariposa.

"Some gratitude," I whisper. She looks nothing like the traumatized lady we saw yesterday. Her flanks are narrower, and protectiveness is all.

"Look how sore his feet still are," Steve says, pointing unnecessarily to the tiny hooves. Like a frightened cat, Mariposa arches his back, and it's clear he's having trouble walking, stepping around his mother as if on tiptoe, and staggering drunkenly to get at the milk. His tongue hangs out miserably, and, all in all, he looks more like a laundry bag than a calf.

But he's alive and nursing, and his sore hooves will heal. If only I'd been handier with the chains. For a moment, he turns his cobalt-blue eyes on me; I am not someone he remembers, but a strange, interested creature, and no threat. Quietly, I sit and watch him as he nurses, and the men get about their business in the other stalls. After lunch, I'll be flying far away from him, but not nearly so far as where he came from only yesterday.

After goodbyes at the cookhouse, Al and I take to the air, to fly me back to Amarillo, where I'll catch a plane to Kansas City, Wichita, Chicago, and points east. Below and behind us, the ranch slides into an airy past. First the habitations disappear (all apricot stucco, the roofs a terra-cotta that matches the corrals), the garages and trees, the creekbed where out-turned horses spend the night awaiting the wrangler's whoop that calls them to early duty. In the slush of an eastern winter, or maybe trapped in a noxious conga line along some interstate highway, I'll think of the ranch's membrane of lives, of people going about their chores in the half-light after sunrise and in the pastels of late afternoon. And, no doubt, from time to time they'll think of me as well: the tenderfoot up every day before dawn just to watch the quality of light change in the corrals, or stopping to roll a bit of sagebrush in her palm, or limping across the room after dinner when, thanks to the democratic fatigue of the body, she was sore in every joint, muscle, and tendon.

As we fly closer to Amarillo, cattle country pours hard and flat as steel. I watch the pastures reel silently beneath us, like the film of some distant event. Soon the blue grama grass will sprout lush and nutritious, and the hibernating insects wake with loud scissory kicks of their legs and warbles of their shells. Looking down on the bean-hard earth, I imagine the life stored within it: grasshopper eggs an inch or so below the surface; harvester ants lower down, away from the frost line;

and beetle larvae tunneled even deeper, nestling along the grass roots. I know insects will help pollinate the grasses by scattering seed, but mostly the ever-blowing winds will do the job.

For Al Mitchell, the grass means the life or death of his herd, and this year it will come up fine and abundant. With winds and insects, it doesn't need a colorful flower to attract a pollinating bee or wasp. When the seeds shimmy loose from the grass heads, they'll blow about, be buried by soil and sand and rodents, picked up on the hides of mammals, and stomped deep into the ground, all by accident, if *accident*'s the word for so elaborate an operation. I fix on a patch of empty land and picture the lush stalks of blue grama to come when I am no longer around.